My Best Jo J
May All your Good Fortune
Be As Numerous As —
"Blades Of Grass"!
.. And Then Some!
　　My Best
　　George P. Some

GEORGE TOMA

Nitty Gritty Dirt Man

GEORGE TOMA
WITH
ALAN GOFORTH

WWW.SPORTSPUBLISHINGLLC.COM

© 2004 George Toma and Alan Goforth
All rights reserved.

Director of production: Susan M. Moyer
Project manager: Greg Hickman
Developmental editors: Gabe Rosen, Elisa Bock Laird
Acquisitions editor: Bob Snodgrass
Dust jacket design: Christine Mohrbacher
Photo editor: Erin Linden-Levy
Copy editor: Holly Birch

All photos courtesy of the author.

ISBN: 1-58261-646-9

Printed in the United States.

CONTENTS

Foreword vi

Introduction viii

CHAPTER 1
    An Amazing Journey 1

CHAPTER 2
    From Coal Fields to Ball Fields 4

CHAPTER 3
    Breaking into the Game 14

CHAPTER 4
    Korea and Back 22

CHAPTER 5
    Up Through the Minors 28

CHAPTER 6
    Goin' to Kansas City 34

CHAPTER 7
    Hail to the Chiefs 46

CHAPTER 8
    Super Bowl Shuffle 52

CHAPTER 9
    Where's the Grass? 68

CHAPTER 10
    Conversion Experiences 80

CHAPTER 11
    Talkin' Baseball 86

CHAPTER 12
    Legends of the Fall 92

CHAPTER 13
Front Office Follies 98

CHAPTER 14
A Kick in the Grass 106

CHAPTER 15
Guten Tag and Aloha 112

CHAPTER 16
Toma to the Rescue 122

CHAPTER 17
Fake Grass, Real Challenges 130

CHAPTER 18
The End of Grass? 136

CHAPTER 19
The State of the Art 146

CHAPTER 20
The George P. Toma Hall of Fame 158

CHAPTER 21
Grass Growing 101 168

CHAPTER 22
Groundskeeping by Deceit 180

CHAPTER 23
And Then Some 186

Appendix A: Resumé 192

Appendix B: Hall of Fame Acceptance Speech 198

Appendix C: Kansas City Sports Commission Speech 200

Appendix D: STMA Open Letter 204

FOREWORD

I joined the Kansas City Royals late in the 1973 season with a lot to prove. The team was counting on a kid who had never hit .300 in the minor leagues to anchor third base as the team set its sights on the mighty Oakland A's in the American League West.

I was fortunate to be around a lot of wonderful players, coaches and managers who helped me hone my skills. But few people have had a greater impact on the way I went about my business than George Toma, the greatest groundskeeper in the history of the game.

How good was George? He could even grow grass on the bald head of Mickey Cobb, our longtime trainer. But ironically, the Royals took the best grass man in the business and handed him a vacuum cleaner, because in those days, Kauffman Stadium had artificial turf.

That didn't keep George from doing his job, however. The dirt around third base and first base where I played was immaculate. And our grass practice fields in spring training were better than any of the major league parks I visited during the regular season.

I wasn't the greatest ballplayer when I came up, but I went into the Hall of Fame with more than 3,000 career hits, a lifetime batting average above .300 and the fourth-highest vote total in history. My secret? Endless hours of hard work.

I take great pride in working myself into a Hall of Fame player, but there was one person I could rarely outwork. When I got to the ballpark to take early batting practice at 4 p.m., there was George Toma, watching from the side. As soon as we finished hitting, he would fix the field and have it looking immaculate for that night's game.

After I retired, I worked as an instructor during spring training in Baseball City, Florida. I would get to the stadium by 6:30 in the morning, and there was George, dragging the infield by himself. George has a term for this work ethic—"and then some." As he always says, that's what separates the mediocre from the great.

That attitude has given George the opportunity to work every Super Bowl game that has been played, as well as the Olympic Games, World Cup soccer and international football games. It also has made him a success off the field with his family, friends and many admirers.

The truth is, George Toma and George Brett are alike in a lot of ways. We couldn't wait to get to the ballpark, and we never wanted to leave. When you have the right attitude, good things can happen.

Nitty Gritty Dirt Man has some wonderful stories about baseball, football and the great characters of the games. But more than anything, it's the remarkable story of a great friend who has lived his life to the fullest—and then some.

George Brett
Mission Hills, Kansas
2004

INTRODUCTION

George P. Toma has a simple philosophy of life and work: "And then some." Simply put, always work a little harder and do a little more in every endeavor.

Toma learned that philosophy growing up in a poor coal mining town in northeastern Pennsylvania during the Depression. His father worked long hours in the coal mines, yet always found time for his family. Although his father died when George was only 10, he has always tried to live up to his example.

Although too small to play sports, Toma loved the sights and sounds of the games and followed the Philadelphia Phillies and New York Yankees and Giants. His neighbor invited him to help take care of the field of the minor league baseball team in nearby Wilkes-Barre. Toma's big break came when Bill Veeck of the Cleveland Indians purchased the franchise. Toma was assigned to help develop a number of minor league fields with groundskeeper Emil Bossard of the Indians, the man Toma considers the best who ever lived.

Despite Bossard's advice, Toma became groundskeeper for the Kansas City Athletics of the American League in 1957. The notorious playing field soon became a showcase. Soccer legend Pele once remarked that it was the second-best field he had ever played on, just behind venerable Wembley Stadium in London. In the early 1960s, the Kansas City Chiefs also began playing at Municipal Stadium. Toma worked for some of the most colorful owners in sports, such as Charlie O. Finley, Lamar Hunt and Ewing Kauffman. Although he had numerous offers to go elsewhere, he has continued to call Kansas City home.

Toma was the logical choice to prepare the Los Angeles Coliseum for Super Bowl I—and the NFL has contracted with him to do every

Super Bowl that has been played. Toma has seen it grow from a curiosity that didn't even sell out that first year to the greatest single day in sports. He also prepares the field for international exhibitions around the world and the annual Pro Bowl game in Honolulu. The NFL honored him with the Daniel J. Reeves Pioneer Award in 2001.

Toma's work has introduced him to the legends of the game, from Ted Williams to George Brett in baseball, and from Vince Lombardi to Joe Montana in football. Yet through it all, he has remained the kid from Edwardsville, Pennsylvania, who has a passion for sports and a drive to give athletes the best playing surface possible. For more than half a century, George Toma has given professional athletes the best he has to offer—and then some.

CHAPTER 1

An Amazing Journey

"The Pro Football Hall of Fame is proud to award the Daniel F. Reeves Pioneer Award to…George P. Toma!"

Hearing those words in Canton, Ohio, on August 3, 2001, took my breath away. The award, named in honor of the late owner of the Los Angeles Rams, is presented periodically to nonplayers who have made significant contributions to the sport. And now, my name was beside names such as the legendary voice of the NFL, John Facenda, who won the award in 1986.

I have a basement full of awards and plaques of all shapes and sizes. I have worked in two Olympic Games, one World Cup soccer tournament, baseball's All-Star game and World Series and every Super Bowl game ever played. I have maintained fields from Tokyo to Mexico City to Barcelona. But for this 74-year-old man, nothing compares with being honored where my boyhood heroes and the stars of today are enshrined in the NFL Hall of Fame.

It's been a remarkable journey for a kid from the coal mines of Pennsylvania, who had to go to work at age 10 when his father passed away. Although that plaque in Canton, Ohio, reads George Toma, I guarantee you that the fingerprints of countless owners, coaches, players, groundskeepers, sports journalists and fans are on it as well. Without them, there would be no Nitty Gritty Dirt Man.

My NFL boss, Jim Steeg, helped me celebrate my award from the NFL Hall of Fame in 2001.

CHAPTER 2

FROM COAL FIELDS TO BALL FIELDS

Ukrainians from the coal mining towns of eastern Pennsylvania may not quote Jewish proverbs too often, but I have found one I love: "Every blade of grass has an angel bending over it, whispering, 'Grow, grow, grow.'"

And so, I am convinced, does George P. Toma. How else can you explain all of the amazing things that have happened to this son of a poor miner, for whom just putting food on the table was a miracle in itself?

My family has its roots deep in the coal mining country of Edwardsville, Pennsylvania, in the beautiful Wyoming Valley near the Pocono and Allegheny Mountains. When the first settlers arrived from Connecticut and settled on the western shore of the Susquehanna River in 1884, it was little more than farmland. But then coal was discovered. The Waterman-Beaver Coal Company (later Kingston Coal Company) opened a breaker there, with a plan to load coal on barges and ship it down the river to the foundry at Danville.

Toma is one of those names that easily can be confused. When I work in Japan or Hawaii, I find that Toma is a common Japanese name, so people often are surprised when they meet me. But my family name is Ukrainian. My mother's parents were Ukrainian and Polish, and my father's parents were Russian and Ukrainian.

I was born on Groundhog Day—February 2, 1929—the brother of Catherine and the only son of George and Mary Toma. Although I have been fortunate to rub shoulders with athletes, team owners, politicians and people from all walks of life, no one has had more of an impact on my life than my father.

Dad worked in the breaker of the coal mine, which was a dirty, thankless job. But for a kid like me, it was a special place, because my dad was there. Although the sights and sounds scared me, when he smiled, I knew I was safe. One time, Dad took me to the circus, and we had to go over the Susquehanna River Bridge in his Plymouth. I was afraid and crying, but he held me close to his heart, so I knew I was safe.

Working in the mines six days a week didn't leave much free time, but Dad did everything he could to spend time with his family. On Sundays, we went for walks and picked berries and clover. Because we had no money, he would make toys for my sister, Catherine, and me. I remember him making us little coal cars from a cheese box and spools of thread.

Dad never complained when he was sick, never bitched to anybody and always did what he could to help people out. I remember he once built a concrete wall for my grandmother. Because the concrete was still setting, he refused to leave to pick up his paycheck at the mine and had to wait another week to get paid. He believed in doing a job right, even if it cost him.

My only regret is that my dad never saw my family nor my success in my career. Dad, like many miners, developed black lung disease from breathing coal dust. When I was 10, we took a walk and came in through the front door of our house. Dad took four or five steps, fell down in front of me and died. I was the last person he ever saw.

I quickly learned a valuable lesson about the importance of family and friends. Although my neighbors were poor like us, they gave what they could to help us get through those hard times. My mother, of course, had to go back to work to make ends meet. She was a small woman—

about five feet tall—but she used to throw those pans around at the Blue Ribbon Bakery. She came home bruised, and her feet would be sore, but just like Dad, she never complained. She sacrificed to give us a better life. If you didn't work, you couldn't make it. We may not have had much money, but we sure had a lot of fun.

Winters are long and cold in northeastern Pennsylvania, and our plank houses were not known for their insulation. You also couldn't see out the windows, because they usually were coated with a layer of frost or ice. About the only place you could stay warm was sitting by one of the potbelly coal stoves in the kitchen or dining room. I can still remember snuggling up to a red-hot stove, listening to my favorite radio programs, such as "The Shadow," "Gangbusters" and "Tom Mix."

When bedtime came, we slept under what the old-timers called a feather tick, which was a homemade pillow the size of your bed, stuffed with goose and duck feathers. Heat didn't travel upstairs to the bedroom, but the feather tick kept us warm. I felt like one of the pioneers.

Grandmother Noosh kept food on our table. She was a wonderful cook. We had potatoes every day, but they were always fixed differently. She raised a big garden, and I loved to visit her cellar. We would butcher a hog and go down to the cellar and smell that bacon and ham hanging up to cure. There also would be chickens sitting on eggs, clucking away.

That cellar looked like a grocery store, with row after row of Ball and Mason jars full of food. There even were strings of mushrooms hanging in the attic to use during the winter. I can still taste that food today, and I am happy that many of the churches in town still serve it the old-fashioned way during their summer bazaars.

My mother and grandmother cooked and baked on old-fashioned coal stoves their entire lives. My mother always kept her stove immaculate. When the valley flooded, as it did every so often, the electricity would go out, and the neighbors would come over to cook on our stove. My uncle John continued to cook on my grandmother's stove right up until he passed away several years ago.

I don't know how we could have gotten along without that old stove. Besides cooking and baking, it helped heat the house in the winter and had a water jacket for boiling hot water. We had to feed it coal and use a shaker to get the ashes to drop into an ash tray. Everybody had a coal bin in those days, with one or two tons of coal stored away for winter.

I still can taste the food we cooked on that stove. We made toast by holding bread over the fire in a wire mesh holder. The holder also worked great for roasting meat over the fire. No offense to Kansas City barbecue, but that was the best meat I have ever eaten.

If we needed something, we found a way to make it ourselves, or we did without it. We had a pump sausage maker to make sausages, which we hung in the smokehouse to cure. We sliced cabbage from the garden to make sauerkraut. We even had a weaving machine to make our own carpets.

Even the simplest chore was a challenge. Right next to my grandmother's house were railroad tracks that would bring up the coal in big cars. Grandma and the other women would wash their clothes and hang them out to dry, then that old steam engine would huff and puff, and all that black soot would get all over the clothes. But that was life, and we never complained.

My uncle Jay Yarrish was another great influence on my life. He and Aunt Eva took me under their wings when Dad died. Uncle Jay was athletics director at Plains High School, taught math and could speak about a dozen languages. In the summer, he painted houses. When you go down the line in life, you remember the people like him who helped you so much.

Few people had a greater impact on my life than my uncle and aunt, John M. and Eva Yarrish (far left).

You have to grow up fast when your father dies. I honestly can't remember a time when I didn't work, and work hard. My first job was at Obritas Grocery Store. The owner's son and I put potatoes in peck bags on Fridays for the big sale on Saturdays, and the owner sometimes treated us to baseball games.

When I was 10, I went to work at Garahan's Farm. We didn't have cars or bicycles, so I walked the two miles to the farm. I had to be there from 6 a.m. to 6 p.m., six days a week, picking tomatoes for 10 cents an hour.

The next summer, I moved up to working on a chicken farm that was four or five miles away, and again, I got there by foot. My job was to clean out manure, gather eggs, feed and water the chickens and tend to the hogs and vegetable garden. The owner also had a little vegetable garden, raised hogs and worked as a milk man. In those days, you delivered milk by horse and wagon to stores and people's homes. I sometimes helped him on his route and learned that the horse was smarter than I was—he knew where to stop.

I earned a whopping 50 cents a day, and the owner provided lunch. He gave me two chickens on Saturdays, and during the week we had all the eggs we wanted. During the summer, he gave us corn, tomatoes, cabbage, lettuce and all of the types of vegetables he grew.

He taught me the value of teamwork, that you always will have people who work and people who lean on that shovel so long that it grows roots. He told me, "George, if you're going down the road with a horse and wagon and you get in a ditch somehow, how are you going to get out?" He said, "You can whip the lazy horse as much as you want, but he's not going to get you out of that ditch. You have to whip the good horse, the worker. He's the one that's going to get you out of that ditch."

If I am leading a grounds crew and have to get a job done in a hurry, sometimes I'll go up to the guys and say, "Hey, I'm going to have to whip you. You're going to have to be the leader, you're going to have to get us out of this jam. Some of the other people are lazy, and they're not going to do it."

Despite—or maybe because of—the hard work, life was great. None of us had any money, but we helped each other out. No one locked their doors at night. Everybody had a couple of chickens, ducks or geese, or maybe they had a hog or a cow.

We had to take the cows about a mile up into the mountains to graze every morning at six and bring them back to milk at six in the evening. I was afraid of the cows with horns, so I carried a long stick. One day, I was bringing the cow back and had to cross the street to get to the railroad tracks. The streetcar came by and scared the cow, and she ran all the way home. I caught hell, because there was no milk. She had lost all her milk running home.

Holidays were always exciting, because our traditions for Easter and Christmas came from the Ukraine, Russia and Poland. What cooks, what bakers, my mother and grandmother were! All of our bread was homemade. The women had a 55-gallon wooden barrel and bought 50 pounds of King Midas flour at a time. They even saved the bags to make clothes. What tomatoes they could grow! People had apple trees, pear trees and vineyards of grapes in their yards.

Halloween was a red-letter day on every kid's calendar. We always did a lot of harmless pranks, such as tipping over outdoor toilets or tarring the toilet seats. We were mischievous kids, but no one ever got hurt.

We even managed to earn a little money along the way. Kids used to go into bars and sing, and the patrons would give them a penny or two, or if they were lucky, a nickel or dime. A coal-mining town like Edwardsville had a lot of bars, so we made out pretty good.

World War II touched our little town, with soldiers heading off to Europe or Asia. When I was young, about 12 or 13, I was an air raid messenger. At night they would have air raid tests, and everybody would have to turn their lights out. We would have to run down the street, knock on the doors and tell people to turn their lights off.

Between the hard work and school, we found time for sports. I have loved sports for as long as I remember, although I was too small to play much of the time. We made up in enthusiasm what we lacked in money.

For basketball, we put up a peach basket, and we used a Carnation milk can for a ball. For football, we used rags stuffed in a stocking. We had one baseball, and it was all taped up. The bat had nails in it and also was all taped up. For our gloves, we took oil cloth that we had on the tables, stuffed it with rags, sewed it a little bit and that was our glove. Maybe later, we got a football if everybody chipped in. You had to blow up the bladder, tie the laces and play. Many of the guys I played with, like Ed Obritas, John Zielen, Frank Kotch and George Hudock, were great friends then and remain so today.

There wasn't much room to play ball because of the coal mines. We knocked down the weeds for football by playing on the field. It still would be knocked down the following spring for baseball, until the weeds grew up again. We used anthracite coal ashes to line the fields and black coal dust on snow-covered fields.

When I was eight, we started building little pitching mounds. We played on rock piles, and our bases were the biggest rocks we could find. We dragged the infield by pulling old bed springs by hand to smooth the field. That was my humble start as a groundskeeper.

I loved baseball, but I was a bit too small to play. At that time, fans in our area followed the Philadelphia Phillies and Athletics and New York Yankees, Giants and Dodgers. Once in a while, we would load up a school bus with kids and go to Philadelphia or Yankee Stadium to see a game. I remember the high school teams traveling to games by standing up in the back of a coal truck. It was a thrill to see players such as Joe DiMaggio and Billy Hitchcock.

Thinking back on those road trips reminds me again of just how much things have changed. Every little town in the Wyoming Valley had its own football team—there must have been a couple dozen of them. When the big game rolled around, the visiting team would load up the players in the bed of a coal truck and drive to the opposing school. Most of the fans didn't have cars, so they usually walked or took the street car to games.

When I was starting out in minor league baseball, most of the big league teams still traveled by Pullman car. Then the Brooklyn Dodgers and New York Yankees took a big step forward when they began traveling by airplane. Today, the teams travel first class, and I think nothing of jumping on a plane to work on a field in Hawaii or Europe. We have come a long way.

I still am amazed at how we made so much out of so little. One thing I know for sure is that relationships are what life is all about. You remember the people who helped you, and there would be no George Toma without the people who helped along the way. Just like that blade of grass, angels were watching over me.

CHAPTER 3

BREAKING INTO THE GAME

Not only were angels watching over me, but so were my family, friends and neighbors. I will always be grateful for the people who stepped up to the plate to help a young boy without a father.

At that time, our neighbor across the street was Stan Schlecker. Stan worked as groundskeeper for the Wilkes-Barre Barons of the Class A Eastern League. Shortly after my father died, Stan started taking me along to old Artillery Park to drag the infield.

Artillery Park was part of baseball lore long before I got there. Babe Ruth played in a exhibition there on October 12, 1926, right after his Yankees had lost the World Series to the St. Louis Cardinals. A baseball historian recently estimated that the home run he hit that day traveled more than 600 feet, making it the longest of the Babe's storied career.

At that time, our high school was only about 300 yards away. Because they didn't have enough classroom space, students went to school in shifts. We would go to school from 7 a.m. until noon for one month, then the other months we would go from noon until 5 p.m. When I went from seven to noon, I would work at the stadium in the afternoons. When I went from noon to five, I would deliver milk. When I was 16, I graduated from high school and started working at the ballpark full time.

In those days, we didn't have the grass varieties that we do today. You had annual, perennial and Italian ryegrass and one variety of bluegrass, plus fescue. Most of the fields had a lot of clover in them. Today, you have a couple hundred ryegrasses, a couple hundred fescues and a couple hundred bluegrasses. We made the most of what we had to work with, and I am proud to say we never had a dandelion in that field. The Italians in our community would come by over lunch break and pick them to eat in salads or make a batch of dandelion wine.

There was no irrigation, so I watered the outfield once with a fire hose. It was in a flood-prone area along the Susquehanna River and right across the street from a coal mine. The 109th Artillery still had horses that pulled their caissons, so a long home run just might wind up in the horse pen.

Today's groundskeepers use biostimulants to help their grass grow. That's a fancy word for what we did in Edwardsville decades ago, which was take cow manure, soak it in barrels of water and spread in on the grass.

Along about 1947, when Bill Veeck bought the Cleveland Indians, he came into Wilkes-Barre and changed the name of the team to the Indians. He told Stan he now was the bus driver and trainer, and I was the groundskeeper. I have to admit I was as green as the grass in the outfield, but I was eager to learn. And thanks to Veeck, I learned from the best groundskeeper who ever lived.

In 1948, he sent me to spring training with Emil Bossard, the head groundskeeper in Cleveland. Emil is the best I've ever seen. He could take a rake and lay out an infield that was right on the money. Emil's sons—Gene, Marshall and Harold—followed him in the business. His grandson, Roger Bossard, is now the head groundskeeper at U.S. Cellular Field in Chicago.

The first place I went with Emil was Driver, Virginia, near Suffolk, the home of Planter's Peanuts. They would fly us 10 minutes from Suffolk out to Monogram Naval Air Station in Driver, which we were turning into a baseball field. I remember the ballplayers driving down the runways and shooting rabbits at night.

With World War II over, we would go into naval stations or army bases in Florida, knock down the buildings and build practice fields. They would use the barracks to house the players and the mess halls to feed them.

In 1949, we went down to Marianna, Florida, to build fields. Emil continued on to Tucson for spring training, while I stayed behind and maintained those fields. In 1950, we went to Daytona Beach Naval Air Station, where the airport is now. Five of us built six and a half fields. Emil would seed the fields, and we had to rake that seed in, pushing and pulling, all by hand. To this day, there is not a machine on the market that puts seed down like Emil did. He would carry a 10-quart bucket and just throw that seed out. It was perfect—no skips or anything. Truly amazing.

The minor leagues were much more extensive in those days. The Indians had 18 teams, and all of them came to Daytona Beach to train. In 1950, we went down to Daytona Beach and watched the automobile races on the beach from the roof of the clubhouse across the street, where we later watched the Daytona 500.

The coaches always tried to come up with new and better ways to teach the fundamentals of the game, such as sliding. Hank Greenberg and I came up with the idea of building sliding pits. I placed pegs in the ground, then attached the bases using strips cut from heavy-duty inner tubes. When players slid into the base, they were on a firm surface. But when they hit the base, it gave way and kept them from getting injured. We used the pits with all of our minor league teams.

As soon as spring training ended, I headed back to Artillery Park, truly one of the great old ballparks in the Northeast and now the home of the Wilkes University Colonels. We also put a boxing ring on the pitching mound, and we had rodeos. Along with the Indians, several high school and semi-pro football teams played and practiced on the field. I can remember Coughlin High School practicing football in right field, its junior varsity team on the infield grass and a semi-pro Eastern League team, the Wilkes-Barre Bullets, practicing behind the bleachers—and we never had to resod like they do today.

I'll admit that some of our techniques were a bit unorthodox, such as drying the infield dirt with gasoline. To this day, I don't know where we got it, because gas was rationed during World War II, with A, B, C and D coupons. We didn't have the big crews, large budgets and modern equipment that we have today, so we found ways to make do. I'll never forget sending the Cleveland Indians a bill for $25 for the rental of one mule and one harrow. I had paid Lesco Barney, a local vegetable farmer, to come over with his mule to harrow our field.

I was fortunate to see some great players and umpires come through Wilkes-Barre. A lot of good players would play for their college teams under their real names, then use aliases to play for minor league or semi-pro teams in those days before the NCAA. I also saw our local boy Pete Gray, the one-armed outfielder for the Elmira, New York, team in the Eastern League who went on to play for the St. Louis Browns. He had a knack for catching the ball, flipping his glove and throwing the ball. I even got to pitch batting practice for a hot young prospect named Rocky Colavito.

Sometimes, I wish I had started collecting autographs back in 1942. I would have an impressive collection today, going back to guys like Ted Williams, Joe DiMaggio, Early Wynn and Herb Score, whom I had the opportunity to warm up.

The Wilkes-Barre Indians were like family to me. Standing (from left) are Marty Blake, now the NBA's "super scout"; an unidentified man; sportswriter Jim Bush; sportswriter Tom Hefferman; Uncle Jay Yarrish; radio announcer Harold Coslett; public address announcer Frank Smith; groundskeeper Hank Golightly; and me. Manager Bill Norman is blowing out the candles. Seated next to him are general manager Helen Tomasic and sportswriter Bob Patton.

Ray Boone, one of the best catchers I have ever seen, played in Wilkes-Barre in the late 1940s. I have always said Ray was the best-dressed player in baseball in those days. I got to know Ray's son, Bob, when he played for the Phillies and later managed the Kansas City Royals. Now, I even get to enjoy watching Bob's sons carry on the family tradition.

Marty Blake was public relations director for our team. He was a sharp dresser who always had a cigar clenched in his teeth. If that name sounds familiar, it's because he went on to be PR director for the St. Louis Hawks basketball team and now is regarded as the NBA's "super scout." Nestor Chylak, the umpire, was from the area and got his start in the Eastern League. He went into the Hall of Fame along with George Brett, Robin Yount and Nolan Ryan in the class of 1999.

And yes, baseball is still being played at Artillery Park. It now is the home of Wilkes University in the Middle Atlantic Conference. A new field was installed in the fall of 2001, and it now features two bullpens, an outdoor batting cage, large dugouts and a press box directly behind home plate.

I honestly believe I would have been happy maintaining the field at Artillery Park forever. But soon there were rumblings of war on the Korean peninsula, and it was time again to pack my bags.

CHAPTER 4

KOREA AND BACK

Americans were getting used to the peace and prosperity that followed the end of World War II. When the conflict in Korea heated up, it took a while to remobilize the war effort.

My draft number came up late in 1950, and I was proud to serve my country. But first, I caught a bus from Wilkes-Barre to Cleveland Stadium to see my old friend and mentor, Emil Bossard. Needless to say, the field looked great for the football game between the Browns and Philadelphia Eagles, even in a snowstorm.

I caught a train to Fort Knox, Kentucky, for basic training. Despite all of the gold in Fort Knox, it was far from ready to house the soldiers who were pouring in. The furnaces weren't working, and the barracks were cold. With all of the black soot, I felt as if I were back home near the coal mines.

After basic training, I was sent to Fort Sill, Oklahoma, for artillery training, then on to leadership training at Fort Chaffee, Arkansas. While at Fort Chaffee, I met a fellow soldier who later went on to play for the Chicago White Sox.

Finally, I shipped out to Korea, landing at Inchon, the site of the famous battle. I served in the 15th Field Artillery of the Second Division, seeing action at Old Baldy, T-bone Hill and Arrowhead Ridge. Remember, the United Nations took the lead in the Korean War, so I had the opportunity to serve alongside soldiers from Turkey, France and other nations. It was a great experience.

I served in the army for two years before being honorably discharged at Fort Custer, Michigan, as a sergeant first

I served in the 15th Field Artillery of the Second Division in Korea.

class. I'll admit that some of the men on my crews over the years may have thought of me as a drill sergeant. But I will always be grateful to the army for teaching me how to lead a group of men toward a common goal.

After fighting in Korea, the only artillery I cared to see was Artillery Park back in Wilkes-Barre. There was only one problem—Wilkes-Barre no longer had a team. The Cleveland Indians had moved it to Reading, Pennsylvania. Hank Greenberg said, "George, you're going to Reading." I said, "No, I'm not. My friend, Denny, is the groundskeeper up there, and he's married and has a family. I'm not going to take his job."

The second choice was not much more appealing—a new stadium in Sherbrooke, Quebec, in the Canadian-American League. But just as I was packing up my parka and long underwear, Wilkes-Barre landed a community-owned team. The New York Giants and Detroit Tigers both agreed to provide players. I quickly unpacked my bags and headed back to Artillery Park.

I can't imagine a minor league team with better people in the front office. Mike McNally, the general manager, had played for the New York Yankees in the Babe Ruth era and always had a great story to tell. Helen Tomasic, the team's secretary, treated me like family. What a great person she was—she became like a second mother to me.

Danny Litwhiler, our manager in 1953, was a future Hall of Famer. Danny had attended Bloomsburg (Pennsylvania) State Teachers College, where the field was named after him, then played for the Cincinnati Reds. The Wilkes-Barre players considered him a "player's manager" who always looked out for their best interests. I also considered him a "groundskeeper's manager" who was concerned about how the dirt, grass and pitcher's mound were maintained.

Danny went on to coach the Florida State Seminoles, and that is where he really made a name for himself. He was sitting at a football game with a chemistry professor in a downpour, watching the ball fly out of the players' hands. Danny and the chemist came up with the idea for Diamond Dry, which also is known as Diamond Dust or Diamond Grit. In baseball, you simply drop the balls in a bucket filled with Diamond Dust, shake them around and they are good to go. That invention landed Danny in baseball's Hall of Fame. Imagine—two guys like us going into Halls of Fame for keeping balls and dirt dry and mowing grass.

Danny Carnevale took over as manager in 1954. If we had a Saturday night game followed by a day game on Sunday, some of the guys on the grounds crew used to sleep in Danny's locker. Bill Norman and Dick Porter also managed the team, and I got along well with all of them.

The former pitcher Lefty Gomez managed the Binghamton, New York, team in the Eastern League at that time. One time he asked me, "What's the name of your dog?" "Prince," I told him—and Lefty put Prince on his lineup card.

A lot of outstanding players passed through Wilkes-Barre, guys such as Sammy White, Whitey Ford, Bob Lemon, Herb Score and Rocky Colavito. We also had several talented African-American players, such as Sad Sam Jones, Sweetwater Clifton, Al Smith, Davey Pope and Harry Simpson.

The war was over, I enjoyed my job and I was beginning to put down roots again in Wilkes-Barre. But as Bill Norman told me, "George, keep up the work, and you'll be in the majors someday."

By the time the 1955 season rolled around, I was offered the opportunity to climb the next rung on that ladder.

CHAPTER 5

UP THROUGH THE MINORS

Making a name for yourself as a groundskeeper is a lot like being a professional ballplayer. You have to work your way up through the system, try as hard as you can and hope you get noticed.

Just as is the case with some ballplayers, there are many fine groundskeepers who for one reason or another never get their shot at the big time. I was fortunate to have good owners and managers who continued to give me opportunities to show what I could do at the next level.

In 1955, I became head groundskeeper and stadium manager at Offerman Stadium in Buffalo, the home of the Detroit Tigers' AAA affiliate in the International League, with Danny Carnevale as manager. It was a beautiful field, although you would never know it until the snow melted after the long winters in western New York.

A lot of great players came through the International League in those days, playing for teams in Montreal, Toronto, Rochester and Syracuse. There was even a team in Havana, Cuba, which must have been a heck of a road trip for teams from cold northern climates. I became lifelong friends with a young Montreal player named Tommy Lasorda.

John McHale, general manager of the Detroit Tigers, and Jimmy Campbell, the business manager, set me up with an apartment right at the stadium. I have never had an easier commute, although it was difficult to leave the job behind when I went home after the game.

I thoroughly enjoyed my season in Buffalo, and I even had a glimpse of things to come. I remember several big tractor trailers rolling into the stadium parking lot to pick up concession equipment from Jacobs Brothers. Their destination was Municipal Stadium in Kansas City, the new home of the Philadelphia A's for the 1955 season.

The Tigers sold the team after my one season and purchased an American Association team in Charleston, West Virginia, for their AAA affiliate. Traditional old baseball cities such as St. Paul, Minneapolis, and Indianapolis were in the league, and the legendary Eddie Stanky was a manager.

We already had a good field in Charleston, which I mowed with a push mower. Once again, I had the opportunity to see a lot of future major leaguers, including young players such as Tony Kubek who were about to become part of the New York Yankees dynasty.

Working in Charleston reminded me of the old Italians who made dandelion wine back in Pennsylvania. One day when I came to work, the city employees who maintained the stadium were in my little shop under the stands, turning copper tubing into a moonshine still. I had to tell them to get the heck out.

Another time, I took a worker named Guy Taxton up into the mountains to get a load of rotted sawdust to top-dress the field. Along the way, Guy said, "George, we have to stop." He pulled over, and he put two dollars beside a tree stump. We loaded up the sawdust, stopped at the stump on the way back and there was a pint of moonshine. When it comes to customer service, the moonshiners of West Virginia were ahead of their time.

With a nice field and good management, I decided I liked living and growing grass in West Virginia. But in August 1957, I got a phone call that would change my life yet again. John McHale called to say he had just given the Kansas City A's permission to talk to me about taking over their field. He told me to go up to the press box and call Park Carroll, the general manager of the A's.

Now, I already knew something about the reputation of Municipal Stadium for having one of the worst fields in the major leagues. Simply put, Kansas City had a really bad field, and even worse, management didn't want to spend any money to make it better. How bad was it? They bought a new tarp for the previous groundskeeper but provided no help to take it off in the hot sun, so he cut the brand-new tarp in half. The team fired him, then laid off his crew.

Before I called the A's, I called my old mentor, Emil Bossard. Emil wasn't one to mince words.

"Son, let me tell you, don't go," Emil said. "I'm in there a few times a month trying to straighten that place out for the manager, Lou Boudreau. There's no drainage or irrigation in the springtime, so it floods you out. In the summertime, it gets so hot that it bakes you out. Stay the hell out of there."

That is when things really got interesting, because I also received a call from Bob Howsman, owner of the Denver Bears, the Yankees' AAA affiliate.

"I'd like to have you as our groundskeeper," he said. "You'll probably spend a year here, then you'll be the groundskeeper in Yankee Stadium."

As much as I admire the Yankees and their great stadium, I have never been a New York kind of guy. In 2000, I helped Rick Cerrone open a new stadium in Newark, New Jersey, for his minor league Bears. Yogi Berra came by to see me. I said, "Yogi, the best thing I ever did was not take the Yankees job. I would have had a lot of money, but I can't wait to get the hell out of here. It's too fast for me."

But at the time, I wanted to keep my options open. I flew out to Kansas City over Labor Day weekend to watch the A's play the Tigers, but the game was rained out. I told

Park Carroll and Bob Wachter, the stadium manager, "This is the worst field I've ever seen. This is a cow pasture."

I caught a plane from the old downtown airport to Denver, then back to Charleston. The management in Charleston said, "George, the best thing for you to do is go to Kansas City. If you screw up, nobody will notice, it's so bad."

Not bad advice. I called the A's and said, "I'll take the job."

CHAPTER 6

GOIN' TO KANSAS CITY

Kansas City has a long tradition in baseball, dating back to the minor league Blues and the Monarchs, who were considered the Yankees of the Negro Leagues. But when the A's moved from Philadelphia, it took a while to make the change from a sleepy Midwestern town into a major league city.

Former President Harry Truman threw out the first pitch at Municipal Stadium on May 6, 1955. The A's beat the Detroit Tigers, 6-2, in front of 32,844 fans, although it certainly did not turn out to be an omen of great success on the playing field. But the team drew nearly 1.4 million fans that first year—four times as many as they attracted in their final season in Philadelphia.

The playing field at Municipal Stadium certainly would have embarrassed many minor league teams. It was unattractive for fans and more importantly, unsafe for players. I had my work cut out for me, and I understood how much effort it would take to round it into shape—if it even could be done.

It was no picnic. I had one full-time person to help me, along with a group of local high school kids whom we hired during the season. Plus, we had to do everything on a shoestring budget, because the front office was so cheap. All we had was a Toro professional mower, an aerifier and an International tractor. We even resorted to hiring a few winos off the street to pull tarps.

We found money where we could get it. We used to gather up broken seats and cardboard from the concession stands, sell it for cash at Cohen's junkyard and use the money to buy seed at Rudy Patrick Seed Company downtown.

I was proud to wear the Tulane green, old gold and white of the Kansas City A's.

We continued to use biostimulants (a.k.a., cow manure) to help the grass grow, thanks to the efforts of Larry Runyan. Larry was the superintendent of a golf course in Garden City, Kansas. He used to go to the cattle cars on the nearby Santa Fe Railroad, load up manure in 55-gallon drums, mix it with water and put it on his greens. He would bring manure to Municipal Stadium when he was in town working on municipal golf courses in Kansas City. Come to think of it, handling manure was good preparation for dealing with some of the front-office people I have met in my career.

Even during the hot, steamy summers in Kansas City, we had to spray a fungicide for disease control only once, and we never sprayed an insecticide. If you want to do something, you can find a way to do it. It all boils down to the people.

But you know what? We turned that field around. In fact, it was bad for only one home stand. In about four weeks, we turned it from an eyesore into an oasis in the desert. It was like playing on a pool table. We had cool-season grasses, then overseeded it with Bermuda grass grown from seed. The infield dirt came from Mrs. Zimmerman's farm. The dirt itself was a mixture of Marshall loam and No. 8 plaster sand from the nearby Kaw River. The sand was better from the Kaw than from the Missouri River, and I always insisted on sand from the Kaw location near Edwardsville, Kansas.

But don't just take my word for it. Even today, players and owners use Municipal Stadium as a yardstick and say it was the best field ever. I owe my success to a lot of hard work, and once again, to the help of a lot of good people.

One of them was Dan Silverstein, who ran the concession business in Municipal Stadium. Dan came to me once in the early 1960s with a plan to help me start a landscaping business. Maybe I should have listened to him, but then again, maybe not. I would be the type of business owner who would tell customers how to plant a tree, and if they still messed it up, I'd replace it for free. I always pull for the underdog, which may not have served me so well in business.

I had the good fortune of meeting Dr. James R. Watson of Toro, who in my book is the world's greatest agronomist. I learned to grow grass by experience, while Dr. Watson taught me his own tricks for growing grass. Together, we were an unbeatable team and remain so today. Tex Champion, a local Toro distributor, also began helping me in 1958. Bob Wachter, one of the best stadium managers, was a big help, and Jack Fette, a Wilson Sporting Goods salesman and NFL official, encouraged me.

I can't say enough about the inner city kids who worked part time on our crew. This was before the civil rights movement, but black and white kids worked side by side as if they were family. Many of them have gone on to success in groundskeeping, like Andre Bruce of the Kansas City Chiefs. A few dozen I have touched are in the NFL, major and minor leagues and landscaping. Others have been equally successful in their chosen fields.

I've never seen a crew work faster. Mel Allen, the well-known Yankees broadcaster, once used a stopwatch to time how long it took from the time the umpire dropped his hand until the crew covered the field. The result? Forty-five seconds. During the fifth inning, the crew could drag the infield, change the bases and sweep the baselines in 28 seconds.

But do you know who helped me more than anyone? Charlie O. Finley, one of the most despised owners in the game. I still consider Charlie the finest owner I ever worked for. The first thing he did when he bought the team was double my salary. The town hated Finley, but what I liked about him is that he took care of the little guy. He never lost the common touch.

I judge a man's character by how he treats people who can do nothing for him. Take the way Charlie looked out for the kids on our crew. Henry Wheat, a legend from the

A's and Royals, used to hold the phone near the radio so Charlie could listen to the game from his home in LaPorte, Indiana. If the kids put the tarp down fast, Charlie would tell Henry to double their pay, take them and any kids they saw along the way to Arthur Bryant's Barbecue for lunch and have Arthur send him the bill.

Late in the season, Charlie gave each of them two weeks' pay to buy new school clothes under one condition—they had to bring their clothes in for Charlie to see. At Thanksgiving and Christmas, he slipped them each $50 if they would sing for him.

When my middle son, Rick, was born, Charlie called me in his office and said, "I understand you had a boy born today. Here's a check for $2,000. I want you to be sure to start his college fund with this check."

Charlie outfitted the crew with sparkling white pants and hats, along with kelly green and old gold shirts. One kid went home, washed his hat in a hurry and his grandmother put it in the oven to dry. It came back the size of a pie pan.

Before long, I had offers to go to work for nearly every ballpark in the major leagues. I stayed in Kansas City for two reasons: I loved the city (the best besides Edwardsville, Pennsylvania), and I appreciated Charlie Finley.

Now, that's not to say Charlie wasn't a little eccentric. First, he constantly tinkered with the ballpark itself. Charlie cooked up the idea of adding a pennant porch in right field, with exactly the same dimensions as Yankee Stadium, which was 296 feet from home plate. The only problem was, league regulations said it had to be at least 325 feet. Ford Frick, the commissioner, and Joe Cronin, president of the American League, threatened Charlie within an inch of his life to remove it.

Finally, Cal Hubbard, the supervisor of umpires, made him take it down before the first pitch on opening day. In its place, we had to paint a white line in that area of the outfield. If a ball went beyond that area, the stadium announcer had to say, "Would that be a home run in Yankee Stadium?"

Charlie also had a thing for animals, starting with Charlie O., the mule. We had sheep grazing beyond the outfield fence on Lamb Chop Hill. Tom Wheatly, who took care of the sheep, had to dress in a shepherd's outfit. We used to paint the sheep black, green, purple and every other color you can imagine. One time Bob Wachter, the stadium manager, held the sheep while I sprayed. The sheep moved, and I ended up painting Bob.

Charlie eventually built a zoo in left field, complete with monkeys, pheasants and rabbits. One day, the person who cleaned the cage didn't get it locked, and six monkeys got loose. We chased them all over with big butterfly nets. We caught four of them and a lady down the street found the fifth one in her garage the next day, but we never did find the sixth monkey.

Another time, Detroit Tiger ballplayers filled a hypodermic needle with vodka, injected it into oranges and fed the monkeys. You haven't truly experienced life with Charlie Finley until you have contended with drunk monkeys.

One last animal story. One time we had Playboy Bunny Day, where we were supposed to let rabbits out of their hutches at second base. Fans would chase them with butterfly nets, tag them and take them home after the game. But after the rabbits got out of the cage, it seemed they would rather make love than run. That was funny.

But all of the animals kept the fans entertained even when the team didn't.

Jim Buffington, who took care of the zoo, eventually worked his way through college. Tom Wheatly, our shepherd, became a school teacher and even appeared on the television show, *What's My Line?*

The one place where Charlie really shined was in ballpark promotions. He used to have Farmer's Night and gave away Brahma bulls, donkeys, pigs and chickens. But things got a little out of hand on Fireman's Day.

Charlie bought two vintage fire trucks down in Birmingham, Alabama, and painted them old gold and Tulane green. We drove them around the warning track before the game, with the announcer telling the crowd how they could win one of them. For good measure, we demonstrated how the pumper worked by spraying the grass.

Unfortunately, we also managed to spray a few Yankees players as we drove past their dugout on a Friday night. They were not amused. The next day, as we again drove past their dugout, we were pelted by everything but the kitchen sink. Frank Crossetti and Bud Dayley led the charge. John Blanchard, the catcher, nailed me with a tomato—come to think of it, that was the best throw he made all season.

The Yankees had brought their own hose and hooked it up to the dugout faucets. We had a water fight until the umpire made us stop. But the Yankees should have thanked us for helping snap their losing streak. After the water fight, they won eight straight games on their way to the American League pennant, with Yogi Berra as manager.

We always found ways to get back at the Yankees. One day, Charlie called from Chicago and said, "Go down to the downtown airport. You're going to get a package of uncut perfume. I want you to take that perfume and scatter it all through that Yankee dugout before they come in tomorrow. I want that dugout to smell like a French whorehouse."

The next day, that's what I did. I scattered it through the dugout. I think it did smell like a French whorehouse... but I smelled twice as bad, because the damn thing splashed on me. I was really perfumed for a long time.

I have nothing but good things to say about Charlie O. Finley. In my long career in sports, I honestly can say I have never met a bad baseball player, a bad football player or a bad soccer player. I have never met a bad owner. But I sure as hell have met some bad stadium managers and people working in the front office.

One kid called Hammer started working in the clubhouse in Oakland for Al Zych and eventually became executive vice president of the club at age 13. Charlie told him, "I'm paying for you to tell me what happens in the clubhouse." Hammer wanted to resign after the players found out, but Charlie said, "You can't. That's what I'm paying you for." Hammer went on to become a famous rap singer.

Another time, a player was reporting back to Finley about what was going on in the clubhouse, and Joe Pignatano, the catcher, brought a large, round box of Swiss cheese, put it on the clubhouse floor and said, "You rats! There's your cheese."

Then there was Babe Dahlgren, who had replaced Lou Gehrig with the Yankees and later became a coach for the A's. He used to bring his two sons to the ballpark for morning batting practice while we were preparing the field for the game. Our guys would be ducking line drives and getting hit in the shin with ground balls. Finally, I said, "That's it, Babe. No more of that."

Babe said, "I'm going to do what I want to do."

I went up to Pat Friday, the general manager, and said, "Someone on my grounds crew is going to get killed." Pat said, "Don't let him go on the field any more."

Later, I had to fly up to Chicago to see Charlie, and he said he wanted me to listen to a tape Dahlgren had sent him. Babe really ripped the hell out of me on the tape.

The story didn't end when the team moved to Oakland. When the A's came back to play the Royals, Babe gave Melvin Duncan, my assistant, a hard time during batting practice. I went down and said, "Hey, Babe, move up, no pepper behind home plate." I pulled a dollar out of my pocket and said, "Hey, Babe, here's another dollar so you can make another tape and send it to Finley. You can make it twice as long." He didn't know I knew about the first tape.

Babe got mad and came after me with a bat. Fortunately, Dick Green, Sal Bando, Rollie Fingers and Catfish Hunter were going to knock the hell out of him if he ever came after me. Those guys protected me.

Charlie was a wonderful showman, and he managed to bring the Beatles to Municipal Stadium during the British invasion of 1964. The stage was on second base, and the Beatles actually dressed in our work area, which shows you how much times have changed. Charlie brought them out through the center field fence entrance on an old Budweiser beer truck.

It had been raining, so I had my son, Chip, put poster board down on the warning track for the guys to walk on. As it turned out, he had perfect footprints of John, Paul, George and Ringo, which they later autographed for him. Ringo even gave Chip his drumsticks. Those items would be worth a small fortune today, except Chip lost them all— along with an autographed jersey from Pele and glove from

Nellie Foxx—when Hurricane Agnes flooded Pennsylvania.

Those were fun times with the Kansas City A's, and I was sad to see the team move to Oakland.

Charlie was always thinking ahead, with ideas such as orange baseballs and a time clock to speed up the game. Charlie gave me an Oakland A's World Championship ring with a clover leaf, the years '72, '73, and '74, the three S's—sweat and sacrifice equals success, and my name on it. The last time I saw Charlie O. was when he called to take Donna, my wife, out to dinner. He was in Kansas City trying to sell the NCAA and NAIA on his idea for a reversed-dimple football.

I'll leave you with a final story that Charlie used to tell. The point is not how great George Toma is but how highly Charlie regarded the little guys like me.

"I had a dream last night about Toma. I died and went to heaven, where St. Peter greeted me at the pearly gates. He read my card and said, 'So you like sports. I'm sure you'll want to see our sports stadium. It seats 500,000.' We went to see the stadium, and it was a beautiful place, with solid gold seats rimmed in platinum and studded with 50-carat diamonds. The field was immaculate, without a blade of grass out of place.

"In the middle of the field was this little man in a white coat. This guy was running around doing everything in sight, making the grass grow here and cutting it there. I asked St. Peter, 'Who is the guy in the white coat?' He looked up, kind of laughed and said, 'Oh, that's God. He thinks he's George Toma.'"

CHAPTER 7

HAIL TO THE CHIEFS

I certainly appreciate Charlie Finley's glowing compliments, but I'll be the first to admit that George Toma is all too human. When I make a mistake, it can be a doozy.

Take the fall day back in 1962 that I will always remember. The grounds crew had a storage shed just past the wall in dead center field in Municipal Stadium, 420 feet from home plate. There was a hole in the roof of the shed where the flagpole stood. That worked fine for raising and lowering the flag during baseball season, but it got a little chilly later in the year.

I was up on the roof covering the hole with plywood for winter when I caught a glimpse of a man walking across the field. Now, unless you are a ballplayer in uniform, you'd better have a darn good reason for walking on my field. I slid down the flagpole like a fireman, ran down to the field, read the man the riot act and told him in no uncertain terms to get off the field.

About 60 minutes later, a long Cadillac pulled up to the stadium. H. Roe Bartle, the mayor of Kansas City (known as "The Chief") called out from the car, "Hey George, come over here. I want you to take these two people around the stadium. This is Mr. Jack, and this is Mr. Lamar."

You guessed it. Mr. Jack was Jack Steadman, president of the Dallas Texans, and Mr. Lamar was the owner of the team, one of the world's wealthiest men—and the man I had just ordered off the field. They were scouting out the stadium as a possible new home for their team.

Lamar and I still laugh about that today, although it wasn't funny for me at the time. As sports fans know, Lamar moved his team despite my rude welcome, and the Dallas Texans became the Kansas City Chiefs.

I welcomed the opportunity to work on football fields again because of the variety. In baseball, where only three men play on grass, the wear and tear is minimal. In football, however, 300-pound men slam into each other and tear up the middle of the field. Plus, football is played in cooler temperatures in Kansas City, requiring a different approach to growing grass.

I first started working on football fields as a kid in Edwardsville. My uncle bought me a line marker. I used to sling it over my shoulder, walk along the railroad tracks to Meyers High School and paint the field for $25. We also had football at Artillery Park in Wilkes-Barre from 1942 to 1950.

Hunt and Finley never saw eye to eye, and I often was caught in the crossfire. The A's had my contract, and the Chiefs were supposed to pay them for my services.

Lamar is a great businessman and knows how to get the most from his investment. He came up with the idea of the Wolfpack, a group of energetic fans on bleachers on the field. The fans had fun, but the bleachers killed a lot of grass. We had baseball, football, soccer, concerts and religious events, but we never sodded the field. Some fields today are sodded between two and five times during a single season.

When first I set up the stadium for football, I put in about 10 rows of extra seats, then an aisle. Lamar said, "No aisles. Look how much money you are taking away from me."

We got pretty creative painting the field, learning as we went along. In the summer, we always had the Milgram Bowl, a preseason game named after a local grocery store chain owned by Les Milgram. I wrote the names of all the players in the end zone with a spray can. We didn't have stencils in those days, so I made a 10-foot by 15-foot wooden frame that I could use for all of the letters of the alphabet.

Lamar Hunt and his friend, Bill McNutt, who runs Collin Street Bakery, a large fruitcake bakery in Corsicana, Texas, would talk about painting logos on fields. I learned a lot from those two men. I still pay Bill one dollar for every Super Bowl—but he keeps sending me his world-famous fruitcakes every Christmas. Not a bad trade, in my opinion.

The Chiefs' logo at the time was an Indian head, which was difficult to paint. Then we started painting team helmets at the 40-yard lines, where teams used to kick off. I'll never forget a game against the Boston Patriots. I had my crew of inner-city kids painting the Boston logo while I went off to do something else. When I came back, they had made the Patriot's face black. I said, "Let's compromise. Let's make the patriot look like he has a suntan."

The city fell in love with the Chiefs, and Sunday afternoons became an event. When the Chiefs scored a touchdown, Bob Johnson rode down the field on Warpaint, the team mascot, with Tony DiPardo, the band leader, riding bareback behind him.

We used to rake the field after every game. We could tell what kind of game it was by how many bushel baskets of divots we got. Most games it was four, but after those rivalry games against the Oakland Raiders, we usually got eight.

The playing field soon earned a reputation as one of the best in football, and Pele said it was the second best soccer field in the world. One season, the New York Jets had a Saturday workout scheduled before the game the next day. Coach Weeb Ewbanks told his players, "Work out on the sidelines. You're not going on this field—it's too beautiful." So they practiced on the sidelines.

But despite our success, the feud between Lamar and Charlie was always simmering beneath the surface. Things came to a head in 1964. Charlie called me into his office and said, "George, you're not working football this year. I'm going to give you six months' pay, and I don't want you around this ballpark. If I catch you around this ballpark in the next six months, I'm going to fire you or the guard for letting you in." We had to move all of the A's grounds crew equipment out of the stadium.

I took advantage of the down time to help out a few old friends. Bob Howsman by that time was with the St. Louis Cardinals. I used to fly to St. Louis, where the team had a chauffeur pick me up and take me to old Sportsman's Park.

I also went down and consulted with the Atlanta Braves, who were preparing to move from Milwaukee to Atlanta-Fulton County Stadium. My old boss, John McHale, was their general manager.

I told the architect and contractor, "We need to put down drainage and pea gravel." They said, "No, it doesn't rain that much down here." They just backfilled it with red Georgia clay, then put down sod with a peat base.

As it turns out, Commissioner Ford Frick made the Braves play in Milwaukee one more season. The Braves and Detroit Tigers stopped for an exhibition game on their way north, and it started to rain. That sod floated into the dugouts. After that, Atlanta tried to hire me every year, especially after it also got the Falcons.

One time, I almost took them up on their offer. I was flying to Atlanta, and who was on that plane but Mayor H. Roe Bartle? He was big and took up two seats.

The Chief asked, "Where are you going, George?"

I said, "I'm going down to Atlanta. The Green Bay Packers are playing the Falcons tonight, and they want to talk with me about taking over their stadium." He said, "Come back to Kansas City, and let's talk with the Chiefs." I ended up with a small raise, but not much.

The truth is, I was the lowest-paid groundskeeper in the majors. Even when I retired from the Royals, I could have made a lot more money somewhere else—and I had plenty of offers—but I loved Kansas City and suffered financially for it.

Jack Steadman stopped me one time and said, "George, you do a terrific job. I wish we could pay you more. When you leave, it will take three men to replace you." And that's exactly what it took.

Thank goodness the NFL was about to step in and offer me the opportunity of a lifetime.

CHAPTER 8

SUPER BOWL SHUFFLE

What do you do if you can't find an NFL franchise to purchase? If you are a young Lamar Hunt, you start your own league from scratch.

Lamar founded the old American Football League, which is why the champion of the American Football Conference each season is awarded the Lamar Hunt Trophy. The success of the AFL forced a merger with the NFL, which led to a wonderful career break.

Shortly after the merger was announced, NFL Commissioner Pete Rozelle visited Municipal Stadium to watch the Chiefs play the San Diego Chargers. After the game, the sportswriters flocked around Rozelle. One of the first questions they asked was, "What is the difference between NFL and the AFL?"

Rozelle responded, "There is not much difference in the way they play the game, but I have never seen a better-kept field than they have right here."

The story hit the news wires on Sunday evening. On Monday morning, Tex Schramm, president and general manager of the Dallas Cowboys, called Jack Steadman to ask if he could borrow our two-man crew to prepare the Cotton Bowl field for their annual Thanksgiving Day game, which would be televised nationally in color. So we loaded up our old 1959 station wagon with equipment, drove to Dallas and painted a star at midfield and "Cowboys" in the end zone. It looked great.

Because of our success, Schramm invited us back to prepare the field for the NFL championship game against the Green Bay Packers. There was one problem this time—

Commissioner Pete Rozelle deserves much of the credit for making the NFL the great success it is today—and for giving me an opportunity to succeed as well.

the New Year's Day Cotton Bowl was played the day before the NFL championship game. We had "SMU" painted in one end zone and "Georgia" in the other—and we had less than 20 hours to change it.

The first thing I said was, "Get me a helicopter. Come down low and blow all of our grass clippings into the stands, and as we paint it, it will help it dry." We painted the team logos and NFL shield, but at about 11 p.m., fog began to roll in. But the good Lord was with us, because the sun came out the next morning, and the helicopter dried the paint in time for kickoff.

Thanks to Schramm, I was invited to prepare the field for the first championship game between the NFL and AFL on January 15, 1967, at the Los Angeles Coliseum. At that time, the game didn't even have a name. Once again, Lamar had a creative idea. His young son was playing with a super ball, and Lamar suggested the name "Super Bowl." The name caught on and now is one of the most recognized names in sports.

With all of the hoopla surrounding the game today, it's hard to describe how humbly it began. For starters, I was able to load all of the equipment I would need in an old three-by-four foot trunk. Today, the equipment is stored in a warehouse in Newark, New Jersey, and shipped to the stadium in two or three semi-trailers. The crew at the Coliseum helped me prepare the field; I now have 20 hand-picked groundskeepers on our crew.

There certainly were no guidelines for how a Super Bowl field should look. I came up with the idea of a football with a crown on it, and Calvin Autry of Calvin Autry Sign Company in Kansas City drew a stencil. We used ice skating rink paint, of all things, to paint the logo and the teams' names in the end zones.

I remember watching the Packers practice on Saturday and talking to a man they called Dad, who had been the equipment manager for years. He and his son talked about all of the various strategies that Vince Lombardi might use in the game. As it turns out, Max McGee, who didn't practice all week and who stayed out late the night before the game, was the MVP.

Just getting to the game on time proved to be a challenge. Lamar Hunt saw me in the lobby of the Sheraton and said, "Hey, George, come out to the airport with me. I have to pick up my wife." Before you knew it, the owner of the Chiefs and the Super Bowl groundskeeper were lost in Watts.

I finally got to bed, and the phone rang. It was Bill Walsh, the Chiefs' offensive line coach, saying, "Come down to the bar, you have to have a drink with me and Weeb Ewbank." But I said, "It's 2 a.m., and I have to be at the field at 6 a.m."

Despite the distractions, the field turned out fine. The only bad thing was that my team lost, 35-10. I was thrilled to be asked back again the following year, and nothing has given me greater satisfaction than working with the NFL. It is my life. All of the games start blurring together over the years, but here are some of my best Super Bowl memories.

Super Bowl IV, Kansas City vs. Minnesota, Tulane Stadium, New Orleans. I learned early on that things don't always go according to plan. For example, it must have seemed like a good idea at the time to send two people dressed as a Chief and a Viking up in a hot-air balloon. The balloon veered into the stands, but fortunately, no one was hurt.

I went back into the tunnel to get a drink just before halftime, heard the crowd roar and came back out to see that a touchdown had been scored. The next thing you know, one of those top-heavy girls from Bourbon Street ran out onto the field. John Birch from the Patriots caught her, and he never lived it down.

The field itself was bad. We covered the wet field with sawdust and wood shavings and painted them green to make them look like grass.

Super Bowl XVI, San Francisco vs. Cincinnati, Silverdome, Pontiac, Michigan. It sure was cold up in Michigan. Because of the energy crisis, we had to turn off the heat at night, so frost gathered on the roof of the dome, just as it would on a window pane. We came in one morning, turned on the heat and the frost began to drip on the 49ers logo just like rainfall. It washed the paint off the artificial turf, so we had to get fans in there to dry it off. You live and learn.

Super Bowl XXI, New York Giants vs. Denver, Rose Bowl, Pasadena, California. The Rose Bowl field is always a challenge, because the Rose Bowl Committee paints the heck out of it for the January 1 game. If you took out a divot, you would never notice it because of the thick coats of paint. But this was the finest Super Bowl field I've ever grown from seed. Coach Bill Parcells made a point of thanking me after the game.

Super Bowl XXII, Washington vs. Denver, Jack Murphy Stadium, San Diego. This game, literally, was for the birds. We had 28 days to get the field ready, so we pregerminated seed for three or four days before planting it. The only problem was, the seed was irresistible to the pigeons and doves that nested around the stadium.

We tried everything, including taking seed up to the area where they roosted. I remembered reading once that airports use fake snakes and birds of prey to scare off birds. Billy Gibbs, the assistant groundskeeper in San Diego, suggested placing dead pigeons around the field. Unfortunately, however, a photographer from the *Los Angeles Times* snapped a few photos of the dead pigeons. The next day's headline read: "George Toma Poisoning Birds at Jack Murphy Stadium." Even Gene Upshaw of the players' union was looking into what type of poison was being used. We had to learn to live with the birds.

I since have learned the secrets of bird control. The next year in Tokyo, we used two radio-controlled cars with sirens to scare them off. And Raymond James Stadium in Tampa used a recording of birds in distress to keep them away.

Super Bowl XXIII, San Francisco vs. Cincinnati, Joe Robbie Stadium, Miami. It started to rain early on Saturday morning, the day before the game, and the rain water from the stands was pouring onto the field. Garry Morris, the groundskeeper, said he had to turn on the pump to keep the field from flooding.

It was time to go back to the hotel, and I told Scott Martin on my crew, "Let's be sure we have the field covered and the tarp nailed down so it won't blow off, then shut off the water pump."

We came back later on Sunday morning, and the tarp was still on. We took it off about noon. Scott started mowing the grass, then came over and told me he heard a rumbling noise on the 50-yard line. I told him to restart the mower, but he said that wasn't what was causing the noise.

We soon discovered what was wrong—the pump was still on, and it was pulling moisture out of the sand root zone, making it the consistency of dry sand. If we ever needed rain, we needed it then.

Both teams practiced on the field on Saturday, and Bill Walsh and Paul Brown both loved it. But hunks of sod were ripped out of the NFL shield in the areas where teams kick off. I was sick, and I just wanted to crawl under the sod. After that game, I made up my mind that nothing—nothing—would ever disgrace the NFL shield again.

Super Bowl XXV, New York Giants vs. Buffalo, Tampa Stadium, Tampa. The Super Bowl crew and another of my favorite local crews, the Tampa Bay groundskeepers, had the field in excellent shape. All of the rehearsals for the pregame and halftime shows went like clockwork, and the field stood up to the wear and tear.

Then Operation Desert Storm started in Iraq, and the organizers quickly switched to a patriotic theme. Rehearsal after rehearsal after rehearsal wore out the logo area at midfield less than 24 hours before kickoff. In those days, we didn't have the large rolls of sod that we have today, so we were scrambling for ideas to get the field ready in time.

At 6 p.m. on Saturday, I said, "I'm going to resod 1,000 square feet of the logo area." As I said earlier, I wasn't going to let anything disgrace the NFL shield again. Jim Steeg, my boss, and the crew said, "You're crazy—it can't be done. There isn't enough time, and there is no sod."

I told Eddie Mangan, "Eddie, the horse and wagon are in a ditch, and I'm going to whip you to get us out. Take a few men and cut out 1,000 square feet of sod, six inches deep because of the sand base. Have the rest of our crew get square shovels and any car or truck they can find. We're going to cut sod."

They laughed, but they followed me out to the University of Tampa's soccer field. Nothing could stop us, not even a locked gate. We rammed the gate. The sod was excellent, and we cut pieces 12 inches square and 6 inches deep. We loaded the last piece at 2 a.m., got the sod laid and painted, and it came out terrific.

Then it was time to face the music. When I got back to the stadium, I told Rick Nafe, the stadium manager, what I had done. I said, "I am ready for jail. Take me." Early Sunday morning, Jim Steeg looked out of his hotel window and saw a large hole in the university's soccer field. Fortunately, the groundskeeper at the University of Tampa was a friend of mine, so I avoided the full penalty of the law.

But again, we did the "and then some" to get the job done right. The NFL logo was not disgraced. Sometimes it's easier to ask forgiveness than get permission.

Super Bowl XXX, Dallas vs. Pittsburgh, Sun Devil Stadium, Tempe, Arizona. The Steelers, representing the AFC, practiced at Scottsdale Community College. Don Follett, now with the Washington Redskins, was on my crew, and we seeded two practice fields and sodded another just before Christmas.

Unfortunately, while we were home for Christmas, the Nebraska Cornhuskers came to Scottsdale to prepare for the Fiesta Bowl. Instead of using their fields on the other side of the gymnasium, they decided to practice on ours, because it was in better condition. When we came back, the field was a mess, and we had to start over. Coach Tom Osborne is a smart cookie—he takes all of his players to the bowl game weeks before the event. Where else could you squeeze in two extra off-season practices?

I don't think it was right after we did all that work to prepare it for the Pittsburgh Steelers, but I guess you have to give Osborne credit. He was getting his team ready for the bowl game and used all three of our fields when they were wet. When Tom later wanted to run around the track, I said, "Take your shoes off. You messed up our fields, now you're going to mess up our rubber track."

We also had a few problems with Sun Devil Stadium. First, we had to send back 13 truckloads of sod because it wasn't cut right. We got the new sod in, put it down and an employee of Arizona State accidentally put out too much biostimulant and killed the ryegrass and Bermuda grass.

We had to pregerminate ryegrass seed two weeks before the game.

I told Don's boss, "You go out around the country and speak on transitioning ryegrass out of Bermuda, and you did a hell of a job." But we all make mistakes.

After practice one day, Emmitt Smith came by with a piece of sod. He said, "George, will you please autograph this piece of sod for me? I want to take it back to Pensacola and put it in my yard." So I got some silver spray paint and I autographed the sod, "To Emmitt Smith, a great ballplayer."

Super Bowl XXXII, Denver vs. Green Bay, Qualcomm Stadium, San Diego. Nothing can test a groundskeeper's patience like rehearsals for pregame and halftime shows. First, they had 44 baby grand pianos on tractors, which rutted the field. Then they had a giant jukebox with Chubby Checker coming out of it. They forgot to use flotation tires, so it got bogged down on the field. They switched the tires in the parking lot, then couldn't get it through the tunnel, because it was too tall. Finally, it broke down at halftime, and we literally had to call in the Marines to push it off the field. (Fortunately, the Marines were providing security at the game.)

Super Bowl XXXIII, Denver vs. Atlanta, Pro Player Stadium, Miami. Greg Norman, the champion golfer, also has a sod farm in Florida. Don Follett and I kept a close eye on the Super Bowl sod at the farm in the months leading up to the game. The first time we went by, it looked fine. But about a week later, there were spots about the size of a half-dollar on one side of the field. A few days later, it was like Grandma's quilt, with different colors of spots.

We brought the turf into the stadium and had to doctor it up with 250 gallons of green dye and overseed it with ryegrass. We went over and over it, and it looked great. Greg Norman flew in with his helicopter to take a picture of the field.

Greg said the problem was transportation shock. I said, "How can it be transportation shock when it's grown up the road on plastic, so there's no shock to it?" When I showed him the pictures at the farm, he said he would check into it.

USA Today interviewed me, and I said it was the second-worst sod I'd ever seen in my 58 years in the game at that time. The worst was at the Los Angeles Olympics in 1984. Greg Norman's turf farm wanted me to retract my story, but I stood by it. People believe they burned the field with chemical fertilizer, or maybe they didn't water it enough. To this day, I really don't know what happened, but that's water over the dam.

We gave them another chance a couple of years later for the Tampa Bay Super Bowl at Raymond James Stadium. I went down there and babysat the turf for two-and-a-half months, and it came out pretty good. Greg didn't like me for my comments, but we got along much better after that. He even threw a Christmas party for the crew at the farm.

Super Bowl XXXV, New York Giants vs. Baltimore Ravens, Raymond James Stadium, Tampa. We had just finished painting the bench area with the team colors when one of the sideline reporters walked right through it. I went over there and gave him hell. I told Greg Gumbel and Phil Simms about it, and they kidded the reporter about it.

On Sunday, we painted a white border all around the field. I was in the Giants' end zone, and I saw this tall, well-dressed gentlemen walking across the field. I started to holler, "Get the heck off there!" But it was Commissioner Paul Tagliabue coming by to say hello and how nice the field looks. The commissioner is a great guy, one who hasn't lost the common touch in today's materialistic world. I admire the commissioner, and I don't know how he and his wonderful wife find the time to do everything they do.

Super Bowl XXXVII, Tampa Bay Buccaneers vs. Oakland Raiders, Qualcomm Stadium, San Diego. Of all six Super Bowl fields we have sodded, this one turned out the best, although it didn't start out that way.

We got our Bermuda grass sod from West Coast Turf, and some of the sides fell off during transportation. It took 12 of us two and a half days to fill in the cracks and make it look right, but we got it done. We later overseeded with Pennington's Jet Perennial ryegrass and Mallard Kentucky bluegrass.

And then there were the logistics of the stadium itself. Qualcomm has only one entrance onto the playing field, which was used by everyone from players to entertainers to television crews. We had to put plywood across the end zone to protect the grass. When ABC was installing two or three tons of equipment in the opposite end zone, we put down three layers of plywood the entire length of the field for the eight-ton forklift.

People who have not been through a Super Bowl week can't imagine how much wear and tear there is on the field. The Saturday before Super Bowl week, about 500 people rehearsed on the field for two hours. They rehearsed for about six hours again on both Sunday and Monday. Tuesday was media day, with 2,000 or 3,000 reporters on the field. Thank goodness we had Wednesday to ourselves. Then on Thursday, there were another 10 or 12 hours of rehearsals. Finally, both teams worked out on the field the day before the game.

Warren Sapp of the Buccaneers came up and talked to me after practice about what cleats would work best. Players always worry about their cleats, but we have a tool that we use to show them how different-sized cleats perform.

Often in San Diego, it gets a little humid around 3 p.m. But the Santa Ana winds off the desert were blowing and kept the dew and moisture off the field. Any other day, there may have been moisture, and the players would have had to change cleats.

We still had to do a lot of work on Saturday night to get the field ready, but it came out great. We had nothing but compliments from the players. One of the big offensive linemen for the Buccaneers came up to me after the game, gave me a kiss and hug, and said, "Great field, George."

That was one of the best crews we ever had. The Buccaneers came out the champions, but the sod also came out a champion. There wasn't an MVP on the crew, but everyone on it was a valuable player.

That was the first Super Bowl in which we had two women on the crew (one of whom was my wife Donna). They did the job—and then some.

To me, the best thing about any Super Bowl is getting reacquainted with old friends. The Oakland Raiders were sitting on scaffolds on the field for their official team picture. When Fred Biletnikoff saw me, he jumped down, ran over and said, "Hi, George. How's it going?" Chuck Bresnahan, their defensive coordinator, also stopped by to say hi. Chuck was on my crew in Kansas City when he was a kid and his dad with an assistant coach for the Chiefs.

When you are a 74-year-old man, it's a pleasure to have guys like Fred and Chuck come up and talk to you.

Black Sunday. Football fans know the great names from Super Bowls past, such as Namath, Montana and Elway. But how many remember a star named Toma?

I had a minor role in *Black Sunday*, the 1977 movie about a terrorist attack at the Orange Bowl. My part was to paint the numbers 4 and 0 at the 40-yard line. Robert Shaw, the star, was to run down the field to the 40 and tell owner Joe Robbie (playing himself) to cancel the Super Bowl because of the terrorist threat. Joe replied, "That's just like taking Christmas away from the kids."

It took a number of takes to get everything right, and I had to paint the field each time. The paint probably was an inch thick by the time we were done. If you ever see *Black Sunday*, don't blink or you'll miss my starring role.

Preparing the field for football's biggest game, with millions of viewers around the world, certainly can be stressful, but we always manage to break the tension. One of my favorites jokes comes at the expense of my good friend, Don Follett. Ask NFL players to name the worst field in the league, and they jokingly will say, "Washington," just to get Don's goat.

When Don was at Sun Devil Stadium in Tempe, home of the Fiesta Bowl, his field was always immaculate, but we told him, "Boy, you have a bad field. You could break a leg in there." Teflon Don just laughed it off.

We joked that when Colorado scored a touchdown against Syracuse in the Fiesta Bowl, Ralphie the buffalo, Colorado's mascot, fell in one of those big holes and broke his leg. We said, "Man, there's the buffalo lying down there, and they had to shoot him right there. They asked all the people to turn their heads, the TV went to a commercial, they shot Ralphie and we had buffalo burgers later on."

We tell this story at Super Bowl stadiums around the country, and people always believe it really happened. But Don is a great guy as well as a great groundskeeper, and he can take the joke. Our crews work hard, and we have fun doing it.

I still am amazed at how big the Super Bowl has become, among fans and even among people who wouldn't know Marcus Allen from Woody Allen. I am forever indebted to men like Lamar Hunt, Tex Schramm, Pete Rozelle, Paul Tagliabue, Jim Steeg, Billy Granholm, Don Weis, Val Pinchbeck and Joe Brown. When I die, that NFL insignia is going to be right on my heart. That's how much I love the NFL.

CHAPTER 9

WHERE'S THE GRASS?

As much as I enjoyed working on Super Bowl fields and consulting for other teams, the Kansas City A's and Chiefs remained my bread and butter.

When Charlie Finley moved his team to Oakland following the 1967 season, no baseball was played in Municipal Stadium for a season. Charlie wanted me to go to Oakland with him, but Ernie Mehl, *Kansas City Star* sportswriter Earl Smith, Mayor H. Roe Bartle and Jack Steadman talked me out of it. Then Ewing Kauffman, a self-made pharmaceutical billionaire, purchased a new franchise. The Kansas City Royals began playing in 1969.

We couldn't wait for the A's to come to town that first year. Charlie used to have a horn from the *Queen Mary* that would sound when a player hit a home run. We decided to blow the horn if a Royals player homered against the A's. Unfortunately, a player for the A's homered first, the crowd cheered for him as a former Kansas City player, and a guy on our crew got mixed up and blew the horn. The stadium manager came down to yell at him, but I told him it was just one of those things. The kid made a mistake.

In 1973, the Royals and Chiefs moved to the sparkling new Truman Sports Complex, home of Royals (now Kauffman) Stadium and Arrowhead Stadium. At that time, the trend was toward cookie-cutter, multipurpose stadiums, most of which since have been torn down. The leaders of Jackson County, Missouri, at that time had the foresight to insist on a design that still would look great more than three decades later. They backed a $43 million bond issue for the Truman Sports Complex, which would prove to be a bargain by today's standards.

The stadium, which seated 40,613, turned out to be the lone baseball-only stadium built between Dodger Stadium in 1962 and the new Comiskey Park in 1991.

I give most of the credit to Cedric Tallis, the first general manager of the Royals. Cedric had a number of great ideas, such as switching the sites of the two stadiums for better siting and introducing many fan amenities that are commonplace today. He also headed off a potential conflict with the players' union, which was beginning to flex its muscles at that time.

Opening night at the new park on April 10, 1973, was one to remember. It was a nippy 39 degrees, and 30,464 fans were there to see the Royals beat the Texas Rangers, 12-1.

At that time, there was no padding on the outfield walls. Marvin Miller, the powerful union leader, set up a meeting with Royals officials to complain. Most of the people in the front office were ready for a showdown, but Cedric said, "Hey, he's the president of the players' union. We have to work with this man. Let's make him feel comfortable and talk over the problem." Here they were ready to fight Marvin Miller, but Cedric said, "Let's work with him." Of course, Cedric was right.

Cedric also was a genius with the product on the field, building the team into division champion in record time for an expansion franchise. It's a shame that he still has not been inducted in the Royals' Hall of Fame.

Thanks to Cedric and team treasurer Charlie Truitt, the sports complex had everything a fan or player could dream of—except real grass.

The fans, it seemed, were more upset about the Tartan Turf playing surface than I was. They came up with bumper stickers and even aerial banners reading, "Let

George Do It!" But I had worked on artificial turf before, and my job was to do what my bosses wanted.

Besides, I still had plenty of grass to grow. I also was responsible for the landscaping at the sports complex; the Royals' spring training fields in Fort Myers, Florida; and the Chiefs' training camp at William Jewell College in Liberty, Missouri. Heck, we even had to take care of the lawn at Ewing Kauffman's mansion in Mission Hills, Kansas.

As I said, I knew a thing or two about artificial turf—and I certainly knew that the new field for the Royals was a disaster. The front office asked me to make a punch list of things that needed to be fixed. I said, "What you need is Mrs. Kauffman and the women from the front office down there to make the punch list, because there are not enough coffee tables in Kansas City to hide all of the bad spots." Of course, I still wound up with the job.

I rounded up the kids I had worked with from Lincoln and Central High Schools in the inner city to give me a hand. I had them walk the field inch by inch and put a piece of yellow tape on any bad spot. We wound up with more than 1,000 pieces of tape on that field. The architects, engineers and representatives from 3M, which manufactured Tartan Turf, laughed their heads off at us. But those kids and I had the last laugh, because 3M had to come back after the season and replace the entire base and turf at their own expense.

That led to the Great Tartan Turf Caper. 3M left behind a roll of turf 250 feet long and 15 feet wide to use for patching. We stored it outside the Royals' clubhouse where trucks turn around. Nobody paid much attention to it, and in a year or two, it was gone.

Herk Robinson, who at the time was in charge of stadium operations, asked me, "Where is the roll of turf?" I said, "I don't know. That's not in my section of the stadium." Herk called in the police to investigate.

As it turned out, it was an inside job. The turf had disappeared a few feet at a time. This ballplayer cut off a piece, then that ballplayer took a piece. The husband of one of the secretaries took a piece to use at home. To this day, I'm sure there are former Royals employees who are practicing their putting on a piece of that old turf.

Whitey Herzog was the first person who really understood what we had with our fast surface, large dimensions and symmetrical design. He played a National League style of ball that took advantage of outstanding pitchers such as Paul Splittorff, Steve Busby and Dennis Leonard and speedsters such as Willie Wilson and U.L. Washington. That earned the Royals their first American League West title in 1976, followed by a heartbreaking playoff loss to the Yankees.

County leaders and the design team also showed a great deal of foresight when they built Arrowhead Stadium, which is just across the parking lot. Many of the design elements that are taken for granted today were considered radical at the time—78,000 seats with unobstructed views, luxury boxes and concrete "corkscrews" at each corner of the stadium to move fans in and out quickly.

The only knock on the stadiums today is that they are situated in a sea of parking lots instead of downtown, where they may help stimulate business. But even that is a benefit to fans who want to get onto the freeways and home quickly after a game.

Although the players and fans had the best of everything, the grounds crew had to make do with what we could find. When the complex opened, we had only one tractor and a Toro Whirlwind mower to maintain 65 acres. I even had to clear snow and ice from the parking lot with an

There are times I have been so busy that I wished there were two of me. That's what we had in this promotion for John Deere equipment.

open tractor for people attending events at the Arrowhead Club. Today, they have beautiful trucks with heating, but in those days you froze your fanny and had snow and sleet hitting you in the face. It was tough, but I got it done, working by myself.

We had a little Ford tractor that wouldn't start one day. A guy named Hilton Hayes, a John Deere dealer from Texas, came out of the stadium club. He said, "George, I'll take care of you." Sure enough, his company supplied nearly $900,000 worth of equipment. But the teams never appreciated the support I got from John Deere. To this day, you can see the beautiful John Deere green equipment everywhere at the sports complex.

I honestly don't know what we would have done without local businesses chipping in. Each year, we received:

- Twenty tons of free grass seed from Jim Carnes, owner of International Seed in Oregon.
- Twenty tons of fertilizer from Anderson's of Maumee, Ohio.
- Biostimulants, herbicides and fertilizers from PBI Gordon of Kansas City. The complex is beautiful thanks to Hal Dickey and Everett Mealman.
- Insecticides and fungicides from John Proctor of Mobay (now called Bayer) of Kansas City.
- Sod from Princeton Turf Farm. Thanks to Dean Schole and Bill Latta.

I used to zip around the grounds on a new Honda three-wheeler. Once, I was on my way from Arrowhead to Royals Stadium and heard a "plop, plop, plop" sound. I looked back in time to see one wheel rolling off toward Royals Stadium. I hit a big tree, broke my collarbone and got beaten up pretty bad. It turns out that a cotter pin had broken, causing the bolt to come loose. I am thankful for Bob Frank, the stadium manager, for inspecting the accident and finding out what went wrong.

I have never met a bad ballplayer or owner, but I've had my share of battles with people in the front office. Herk Robinson, vice president of stadium operations and later general manager for the Royals, and I are great friends, but we had a number of memorable skirmishes. For example, Herk would raise hell if the scoreboard operators put my picture on the JumboTron.

One day Herk told me, "You're spending too much time on that field. The way you are sweeping it, you're going to wear it out." I said, "No, we're getting the dirt out of it. That's what's going to wear it out." I was right. Across the parking lot at Arrowhead, the kids on the crew cleaned the turf, filled the cracks and patched it with yarn after every game, and it lasted for 13 years.

The Royals started winning about the time they moved into their new ballpark and dominated the American League West until the mid-1980s. I loved the managers and players I was fortunate enough to work with.

Whitey Herzog was a character, as well as a great manager. When he came to the Royals, he told me, "Hide the damn batting cage. If they can't hit by August, they're not going to hit at all. The only reason they take batting practice is so the hitting coach can show the general manager he's doing his job." I think the reason I liked Whitey so much is that I have some of Whitey in me.

Dick Howser and I had been friends for years, dating back to his days as a player for the Kansas City A's and the New York Yankees. When he left the Yankees to coach at Florida State, he called and said, "You're going to be my groundskeeper." I turned him down, and a few months later, he was named manager of the Royals. I said, "Look, Dick, [if I had taken the job] I would be down there at Florida State, and you would be up here."

Dick sometimes would get tired of talking with the press. When I walked by, he would say, "Come on, George, let's go check the bullpen," or something. We would go in my office and shoot the breeze.

One time in a game at Royals Stadium, Dick looked down the bench and said, "Quirk, pinch hit!"

George Brett said, "He can't pitch hit."

"Why?" Dick asked.

"Look at second base," George said. There was Jamie Quirk, dressed in a grounds crew uniform cleaning around second base. We had a lot of fun in those days.

Brett was the finest baseball player I have ever seen, but we also had great characters such as Amos Otis, Marty Pattin and Dan Quisenberry. Amos use to hide a $20 bill just in the crack in the padding in right field so the grounds crew could search for it. Every Sunday, Quiz took up a collection in the bullpen, and they would hide $100 for the crew to find. One time, they hid it in the chewing tobacco, but the kids still found it.

I can't say enough good things about the way the players treated my crew. Pitcher Ray Sadecki used to bring in that good Polish sausage made in Kansas City, Kansas. Tom "Flash" Gordon gave the crew $100 for barbecue and pizza whenever he came back to town. And Wally Joyner bought two television sets for the crew.

Even our suppliers pitched in. Jim Carnes, who owned International Seed, always showed up with barbecue for the kids, with enough left over for the next day's meal.

I always tried to impress upon the crew that everything they did was for the ballplayers. For example, when Jeff King played first base for the Royals, he wanted the dirt at just the right level of moisture. One day Jeff told the crew, "Hey, a little more water here!" One of the crew muttered something about "high-priced, high-maintenance" ballplayers. I shut the water off and said, "If it weren't for Jeff King, you wouldn't have a job. And what does he want? Maybe five or 10 seconds of water." Word gets around the league, and you don't want a bad reputation. Do everything you can for the ballplayer.

I even loved our long-time trainer, Mickey Cobb. On a bet, I once grew grass on his bald head. We called it a grass toupee. We just took a little cotton, some seed, our special fertilizer and there it was. Hey, it looked pretty good on him.

People in the front office told me the biggest mistake the Royals made was firing Mickey.

Back in the 1970s, I began tossing pieces of bubble gum to a young woman who seemed to be at every game. That woman, Donna, and I were married on February 6, 1981, after the Pro Bowl game in Honolulu. I will let Donna explain why she married me: "I used to tell him I married him for free tickets and parking. I also knew I wouldn't have to make dinner every night."

Our son, Ryan, was born in 1983 and practically grew up at the sports complex. Catcher John Wathan, his godfather, used to spoil him. John brought him a present after every road trip, as well as for his birthday and Christmas. One time, he bought Ryan a motorized Indy 500 car that he drove around the warning track. Bo Jackson bought him a present when he turned nine—a $200 race car set with the blue of the Royals and the black and silver of the Oakland Raiders.

I am forever grateful to the bullpen pitchers and catchers for teaching Ryan how to walk and potty-training him. They deserve an award.

The highlight of my career with the Royals was beating the St. Louis Cardinals in seven games to win the 1985 World Series. People swarmed all over the field, and I remember Ryan crying, "Get off my daddy's field!" I also remember Cookie Rojas and Freddie Patek diving over the right-field fence and into the fountains. They are lucky they didn't get electrocuted with the electricity up there, but they sure had a good time.

The Royals began going downhill after losing good people such as Cedric Tallis, John Schuerholz and Lou Gorman. I heard a story that the mother of Pat Sheridan, a former outfielder, got mad at the Royals and put a curse on them. But maybe the new team of owner David Glass, general manager Allard Baird and manager Tony Pena is beginning to restore the faded glory. It would be great to work under this lineup and positive new attitude.

CHAPTER 10

CONVERSION EXPERIENCES

I often have said that George Brett is the finest baseballplayer I have ever seen. As Whitey Herzog once remarked, George played the game the way the old-timers *think* the old-timers played.

However, the hard artificial surface at Kauffman Stadium took its toll on George's knees and the rest of his body. George once told me that the carpet was good for his batting average but bad for his body. I can only imagine what kind of career numbers George would have put up without losing all of those games to injuries.

When George retired after the 1993 season and moved into the front office as vice president, the fate of the old carpet was sealed. The team's board of directors decided to convert to bluegrass for the 1995 season and reconfigure the outfield fences while they were at it. I was named director of turf design for the project, and my old mentor, Dr. James R. Watson, was the agronomist.

As you may recall, a players' strike ended the 1994 baseball season prematurely and even led to the cancellation of the World Series. The one silver lining in that dispute was the opportunity to get a jump on the field conversion while the Kansas City weather was still favorable.

Our crews worked around the clock through the fall to rip out the old carpet, move in the fences and install irrigation and drainage systems. One of the main reasons for having an artificial surface all those years was that it would drain better, resulting in fewer rain-outs for fans who drove from across the Midwest. But we solved that problem by building a 14-inch root zone that was 85 percent sand and 15 percent reed sedge peat.

I was honored to throw out the first pitch on opening day after Kauffman Stadium was converted to natural grass.

I looked around the nation for sod that would be durable and stand up to the weather extremes common in Kansas City. I found what I was looking for at the Randy Graff Turf Farm in Fort Morgan, Colorado. The sod we selected was composed of five Kentucky bluegrasses: 20 percent Princeton, 20 percent Eclipse, 20 percent Suffolk, 20 percent Nassau and 20 percent Glade. It also contained five ryegrasses: Derby, Supreme, Regal, Gator and Top Hat.

The new field was a hit with the players, fans and front office. It's hard to believe the Royals have been playing on grass for nearly a decade now. My successor, Trevor Vance, and his crew, keep the stadium looking as good—or even better—than the day it opened. I am proud to say that a time when a lot of the older ballparks have been torn down, Kauffman Stadium just keeps getting better with age. There is simply no better place to be on a warm summer evening.

Across the parking lot, the Chiefs also made the move to grass. They had invested a great deal of money in such veteran players as Joe Montana and Marcus Allen and wanted to keep them healthy.

Arrowhead also remains one of the most beautiful stadiums in the NFL, but it needed to keep up with the latest technology. Converting to natural grass provided a great opportunity to take care of a few problems with the original design. To improve sight lines, the field was lowered by six inches along the sidelines, and elevated just 12 inches in the center, compared to 18 inches on the old field. It also was laser-graded to ensure proper irrigation and drainage.

It's remarkable to consider what was installed beneath the surface after 9,000 tons of dirt were hauled away:

- Five miles of electrical conduit to facilitate everything from video boards to sideline reports to rock concerts.
- Two miles of drainage pipes.
- One mile of irrigation pipe.

Layered over the subsurface is a four-inch pea-gravel base, topped by a 12-inch root zone. The root zone is composed of 5,000 tons of 85 percent sand and 15 percent reed sedge peat, just like the one at Kauffman Stadium.

Marty Schottenheimer, who was head coach of the Chiefs at the time, lobbied hard for Bermuda grass, even though Kansas City is on the extreme northern edge of the growing zone for this warm-season variety. Schottenheimer believes it stands up to game conditions better than other grasses, although it must be overseeded with rye as early as October. The Bermuda sod was treated with Panacea steroid to promote strength, then with Bovamura.

With the success of the Royals and Chiefs, it's sometimes easy to forget about Kansas City's other outdoor team, the Wizards of Major League Soccer. The team, also owned by Lamar Hunt, plays an exciting brand of soccer and won the league championship in 2000.

The Wizards also play at Arrowhead, putting the Bermuda grass to good use during the hot summer months. The challenge for Andre Bruce and his crew is when the Wizards play a Saturday night game, followed by a Chiefs game at noon on Sunday. The crew has to scramble to repair damage, mow, replace the soccer goals with football goalposts and repaint. Their job is made somewhat easier with a water-soluble paint for soccer that can be hosed off after the game ends.

Although my work takes me around the world, I never miss a chance to visit Kauffman and Arrowhead Stadiums when I am home and the teams are playing. My crews in the 1970s, 1980s and 1990s started a tradition of excellence at the Truman Sports Complex. I love to see the fans remain in their seats after the fifth inning just to watch the crew sprint onto the field and drag the base paths.

I am proud that the groundskeepers who have followed in our footsteps are upholding our tradition of excellence—and then some.

Being around baseball and football gave me the best seat in the house for some unforgettable games and a chance to meet some wonderful people. Let me tell you about a few of them.

Chapter 11

Talkin' Baseball

Baseball has been my first love ever since I was a kid back in Pennsylvania. We used to play for hours on those rocky fields, using whatever we could find for a ball and bat.

There were few things better than listening to a game on the radio on those hot summer nights. And best of all was when they used to load the school kids up on a bus and take us to a game in Philadelphia or New York.

I have seen thousands of ball games and gotten to know hundreds of ballplayers over the years. Here are some of the memories of the people in the game that have stayed with me.

Ted Williams. I got to know Ted both as the great slugger for the Boston Red Sox and as the manager of the Texas Rangers.

One thing I always do in all of my batting cages is provide double netting as a safety precaution. The coaches can stand right next to the cage without worrying about getting hit. Ted would always come up to me and say, "Thanks, George, for double netting. I like to teach hitting to my players in your ballpark, because I feel safe around your cage. I want to have my groundskeeper do that."

Ted liked it, and he always praised me for it.

Mickey Mantle. Mickey would bitch a little bit because we kept center field hard, because he had bad knees.

Harmon Killebrew. Harmon couldn't field too well, but he sure hit the hell out of the ball. We kept the third base area hard for his aging legs, but he got back at us by putting a lot of shots into our center field shed at Munici-

Even the groundskeepers have to get back into the swing of things at spring training. Here I am taking a little batting practice in Baseball City, Florida.

pal Stadium. I was happy to see him wind up his great career playing designated hitter for the Royals.

Tony La Russa. I had a chance to meet guys like Tony, Bobby Cox, Don Zimmer and Johnny Pesky as players, and they went on to become outstanding managers.

Ozzie Smith. I remember Ozzie Smith jumping over the fence once just to say hello to me. I appreciated that.

Eddie Finger. Eddie was a barnstorming softball pitcher who performed as "The King and His Court," with just one or two players on his side. I gave Eddie Finger the finger once in front of 30,000 people at Municipal Stadium when he was going to dig a hole in the infield before the game.

Jim Fregosi. Jim called me in to build a pitching mound in Veterans Stadium when the Phillies played in the World Series. Veterans Stadium always was a bad field—the Astroturf was dirty and poorly maintained. We went in there and built a mound for them, and Jim and the players were happy.

Minnie Minoso. Minnie was playing for the Cleveland Indians' farm team in Oklahoma City, the bases were loaded and the manager flashed the take sign. But Minnie didn't take—he hit a grand slam.

He came back to the bench, and the manager said, "Didn't you see the take sign?" Minnie said, "Me take—me take for four."

Jim "Catfish" Hunter. Charlie Finley gave him the nickname "Catfish" when he signed with the A's. In those days, players had to spend one year in the major leagues—they couldn't assign you out. That next fall, Catfish had a hunting accident and was sent to Mayo Clinic to get shotgun pellets removed from his leg.

When he got back to Kansas City, Finley didn't want him hanging around the veteran players, so he spent time with the grounds crew. We showed him how we would doctor up the pitching mound and baselines. So when the team moved to Oakland and Catfish came back, he couldn't win a game against the Royals. He also struggled after joining the Yankees. Finally, George Steinbrenner accused us of doctoring the pitching mound and making him slip. He even had the umpire watch the bullpen mound on the day

Catfish pitched. We always had that psychological edge on Catfish, and that edge was a putty knife.

Catfish was one of my greatest friends, and I miss him.

Roger Clemens. The first game he pitched for the Yankees was against the Royals in Baseball City, Florida. National newspapers reported that he would not talk to anyone before the game except Royals groundskeeper George Toma.

Billy Martin. Billy liked to barnstorm back north through Kansas City. The spring training infields in Florida were bad at that time, and it gave him an opportunity to break some bad habits. Wherever Billy went as a manager, he had me come in and check out the infield.

Alex Rodriguez. A-Rod tried to get me to come down to Texas and work the infield at 73 years of age. He could afford to pay part of my salary just for the tax write-off.

Cal Ripken Jr. Cal and some of the other Orioles players liked the Royals' field so much that they would come out and watch us work. They wanted me to write up a program for their groundskeeper in Baltimore so they would have a great infield like we had. I said, "No, you have a great groundskeeper there, let him do it." Cal and his dad, Cal Sr., are two of the best, in my book.

Bret Saberhagen. I'm in my office, and I can hear him coming down the tunnel. I don't know where he got his energy. What a great pitcher, and what a great competitor. Bret was in high gear all the time.

George Brett. George is the greatest ballplayer I've seen in my time. I've seen Ted Williams, Joe DiMaggio and those people, but George was the best.

I like the way he hit, the way he hustled, the way he played. When we had artificial turf, he chewed tobacco, but he never spit on the grass. He would always take 10 or 15 steps and go spit in the dirt.

I have seen thousands of baseball players in my 60-plus years in the game, and George Brett was the best of the best.

In today's materialistic world, he didn't lose his common touch. We had a kid on our crew who was taking a girl to the high school prom. George called up his wife and asked, "Can we give Johnny the Mercedes tonight?" So Johnny went to the prom in George Brett's Mercedes.

George is the type of player I love the most, and he also is my favorite ballplayer and person. I love this man.

I could go on and on about the players I've met—such as Joe Torre, Hal McRae, Bob Boone, Lou Piniella and Jack McKeon—and how well they have treated me. Don't believe the people who tell you how much better the game was back in the good old days. Baseball is better now than ever, and today's players can hold their own with the best.

I know. I was there.

CHAPTER 12

LEGENDS OF THE FALL

My earliest memories of football were listening on the radio to the great army teams with Doc Blanchard and Glenn Davis—Mr. Inside and Mr. Outside. We also saw some outstanding college and semi-pro talent in Pennsylvania, which remains a hotbed for football.

But none of us in those days could have begun to imagine how popular the NFL would become. I am eternally grateful that Lamar Hunt moved his team from Dallas to Kansas City and that the league has trusted me with its showcase game, the Super Bowl. Lamar, Pete Rozelle, Paul Tagliabue, Tex Schramm, Bill Granholm and Jim Steeg always will be at the top of my list.

Just as in baseball, there are football people I will remember forever.

Ronnie Lott and Eric Wright. I was called in to fix the field for an NFC championship game between the San Francisco 49ers and Washington Redskins. I was standing on the 20-yard line during the game, and Ronnie and Eric left the bench area and came down to talk. They said, "How's the crew? How's the family?" I said, "Get out of here—you're going to get fined." I love guys like that.

Billy Granholm. Billy was my boss for at least 30 Super Bowls. Oh, what a sweet man. He said, "George, do the job. We have to spend the money to do things." One time he said, "You're always worried about going over the budget. Try to keep it close, but look at all these rich owners. They are going to drink the best and most expensive whiskey and then piss it away." I would have loved to have had Billy as an owner.

Jim Steeg. Jim took over for Billy Granholm as senior executive vice president of the NFL in charge of special events. I consider him one of the finest men I have ever worked for. My father, my uncle John Yarrish, and then Jim are the best men in my life.

Hank Stram. Hank parked his car in the tunnel all the time and didn't give a damn about anybody. It was Hank's way—he ran the show. He's a funny type of guy. He was a George Toma, and I'm a Hank Stram. We wanted to do what we wanted to do.

One time, Hank gave three game balls away—offense, defense and special teams. Jack Steadman, the team president, got mad and wrote a note saying there would only be two game balls. So the next game, Hank gave out 40 game balls.

Frank Ganz. Although Frank didn't enjoy a great deal of success as a head coach, he was a legendary motivator on special teams. He even talked to the players about how I was able to get the job done when I didn't have everything I needed to work with.

Tony Dungy and Herman Edwards. I went to check our practice field for the Super Bowl in Tampa, and who was ready to go on the field but Tony and Herm.

They said, "George, how's everything going?" I said, "I'm just here to check the field, they won't let me go on it." But they corralled me at the middle of the field with them to watch the team practice. And now, both of them coached teams to the playoffs after the 2002 season. They are two excellent coaches who haven't lost the common touch.

Ben Davidson and Tom Keating. I was working at the Chiefs' practice field by myself in the off season and heard motorcycles coming up the road. I said, "Holy cow, that must be Hell's Angels. What's going on?"

My back was to the gate. All of a sudden, I turned around and there were two motorcycles coming down the center of the field. These guys were big, and I was scared. They took their helmets off, and one was Ben Davidson and the other was Tom Keating of the Oakland Raiders.

I said, "What the heck are you doing here? Get off the grass." They said, "George, we're going cross-country and just wanted to come by and say hello to you."

Ben Davidson, even though he knocked the heck out of Lenny Dawson, is still one of my favorite guys, and so is Tom Keating.

Jim Schaaf. Jim was an outstanding football player at Notre Dame. We started out together working for the A's, then he became public relations director and later general manager of the Chiefs. Jim and I got along great. Jim did a good job, but he could have had more success if he had the kind of money that Carl Peterson has to spend today.

Tony Gonzalez. Tony, who may become the best tight end ever to play in the NFL, and I appeared together in a TV commercial for ESPN. In the spot, ESPN decides to put natural grass in the studio. The crew comes through on a mower, the sprinklers turn on and one of the announcers falls and gets grass stains on his pants. Coach Brian Billick says to take it out with hot water, and Tony recommends lemon juice.

Later, I told Tony, "I'm five foot four and 73 years old, and I got the lead role. You're tall, dark and handsome, and all you say is 'lemon juice.'" We had a lot of fun making that commercial.

John Elway. My son, Ryan, and I were standing in the end zone in San Diego watching Elway against the Packers in the Super Bowl. He had to make that first down. You could see in his eyes when he had the ball that he was going to do it or die trying. He gave his life for that first down. That was a great player, playing a great game.

Jerry Jones. After the Dallas Cowboys won the Super Bowl, the NFL threw a big party at Treasure Island in Orlando. I was working for the Royals at nearby Baseball City, and Jim Steeg from the NFL invited me to the party. Who came by but Jerry Jones, and he stopped by the table with Jimmy Johnson.

Jerry said, "Let's have a toast for the world champion Dallas Cowboys." Nobody raised their glasses. Jerry got mad, went back to the hotel, had a press conference, and that was the end for three Cowboys coaches.

Chuck Bresnahan. Chuck was on my crew at Arrowhead Stadium when his father was an assistant coach for the Chiefs. Now, Chuck is defensive coordinator for the Oakland Raiders. It was like a homecoming when I saw him at the Super Bowl in San Diego in 2003.

NFL coaches. I have gotten to know a number of fine coaches in my years in the game. Among my favorites are Hank Stram, Paul Wiggin, Don Shula, Marty Schottenheimer, John Madden, Weeb Ewbank, Bill Parcells, Chuck Noll, Mike Cavenaugh, Mike Ditka, Tom Flores, June Jones, Walt Michaels and Bill Walsh.

NFL players. Some of my favorites from the Chiefs and other teams are Ed Budde, Jim Tyrer, Buck Buchanan, Bobby Bell, Willie Lanier, Howie Long, Jan Stenerud, Nick Lowery, Jack Rudnay, Len Dawson, Emmitt Smith, Brett Favre, Marcus Allen, Mike Garrett, Deron Cherry and Tom Condon.

I have met hundreds of players, and it's hard to remember all of them without seeing the name or number on their uniform. But it's still a thrill when they come up to say, "Thanks for a nice field," as both the Raiders and Buccaneers did at the 2003 Super Bowl.

NFL officials. I was walking out the tunnel to the playing field at Aloha Stadium one time and noticed these words on one of the doors: "Officials' Room"—in Braille. Now does Braille on the officials' door tell us something about the quality of their work?

Now I can get on my favorite referees: Jack Fette, Art McNally, Red Cashion and many more. I could go on with stories about guys like Brett Favre, who went out of his way to get an autographed hat for me to give the mayor of Nashua, New Hampshire. He forgot to give it to me after a game between the Packers and Saints but sent it to Mike Davidson, the Chiefs' equipment manager, to be sure it got to the mayor. Who ever said players are bad?

Thanks to some wonderful people, the NFL has been great to me. The NFL is my life.

CHAPTER 13

FRONT OFFICE FOLLIES

As much as ballplayers and managers make my job a pleasure, some people in the front office can make it a pain.

Overall, I have gotten along great with team owners. Most owners have been highly successful in their other businesses, which gives them the luxury of owning a professional team. They understand the importance of hiring good people, giving them the tools they need and staying the heck out of the way.

The front office staff can be another story. Many are trying to climb the corporate ladder and impress the boss by berating low-level employees and slashing costs. Unfortunately, the little guys suffer—like when our grounds crew made do with what little we had while the Royals spent millions on free-agent busts. Where was the front office leadership?

I already have told you about two of my favorite owners. Bill Veeck believed in me enough to make me the groundskeeper at Artillery Park in Wilkes-Barre when I was still a senior in high school. And Charlie Finley, for all of his quirks, treated everyone in the organization with dignity and respect. He used to throw a steak dinner for the local and traveling sportswriters about once a week, and he never forgot to invite the guys on my crew, many of whom probably couldn't afford a steak.

When Charlie moved the A's to Oakland after the 1967 season, Ewing Kauffman brought an expansion franchise to town, the Kansas City Royals. Kauffman, fondly known as Mr. K, was as unassuming as Finley was brash. He poured millions of his own money into bringing a world championship to the city in 1985, and the city showed its gratitude by renaming the stadium in his honor. I owe a lot to Mr. and Mrs. K, who never lost the common touch.

Mr. K and I got along fine, because he was always approachable. He did a lot for me, but I also did a lot for him. When Kauffman bought the Royals, we got not only him, but also his family and his mansion in suburban Mission Hills, Kansas.

In addition to Royals Stadium, my crew took care of his lawn. We didn't mind, but we got taken advantage of a few times. Harold Myers, whom everybody loved, came back one day and said, "George, you lied to me. You said all I had to do was take care of Mr. K's house. Well, he also has me taking care of the house of one of his executives from Marion Labs. I don't mind going over there to cut grass as you told me, but they have me babysit, clean the pool and even defrost the freezer."

I talked to Mr. K's chauffeur, Blanchie, and got it straightened out. Sometimes, you do a favor for someone and get taken advantage of. It's not right.

I loved Mr. K's wife, Muriel. One of the highlights of Royals games in the 1970s was the seventh-inning stretch, when Ewing and Muriel would step out of their suite wearing royal-blue suits and wave at the fans. My middle son, Rick, used to shine her silverware when he was 13. They would send letters thanking him for doing a good job.

When Mr. K. bought the Royals, all I knew was that he had two daughters, Julia and Susie. On opening day, I went to the clubhouse to check on the batting practice schedule for the next day. Coming down the tunnel was a man in a soldier's uniform. I said, "I'm sorry, sir, but you can't come up here. You have to go around to the front."

He said, "I'm Larry Kauffman, Mr. Kauffman's son." I said, "Yeah, so am I." I never knew he had a son. But Larry and I became really good friends after that and joked about what I said. Larry, a down-to-earth man, has since passed away.

Julia and I had our moments. The Yankees were in town for the playoffs, and before the game, I was chatting with Reggie Jackson behind home plate. Now, Reggie and I had known each other since he signed with the A's and played at Municipal Stadium.

But Julia saw me, ran to Herk Robinson and said, "Hey, you have to fire George Toma. He's talking with the enemy." Some people just don't understand sports, I guess. The late Haywood Sullivan of the Boston Red Sox and Spec Richardson of the San Francisco Giants had to explain to Julia that it was OK for me to talk to visiting players. And if I had a dollar for every time someone said, "Fire George Toma," I could own a team.

Stadium managers can make or break the groundskeeper. I have worked for some who were really good, like Jay Hinrich, George Humphries, Bob Frank and Bob Wachter, and some bad ones, such as Tom Folk. Humphries was a great engineer, and Frank kept that stadium spotless, but Hinrich was the most dedicated stadium manager and assistant general manager I've ever seen. He is now with the athletics department at the University of Kansas.

I also have sparred off and on for years with Herk Robinson, who was vice president for stadium operations and later general manager of the Royals. Herk is a great guy but finicky. For example, the ballplayers would want to grow tomatoes in the bullpen, and he wouldn't let them.

Herk also gave a strict order that no thermometers be allowed on the field, because it usually was 30 or 40 degrees hotter on that artificial turf. So the ballplayers would bring their own thermometers out there, just for fun and to irk Herk.

The grounds crew caught its share of Herk's wrath. After the 1978 season, we were getting ready for the playoffs and waiting to see if we would play the Yankees or the Boston Red Sox. Just for fun, we put a question mark on the outfield grass where the Yankee or Red Sox logo was to go. Herk went nuts and said, "Get that damn thing out of there!" We listened on the radio as Bucky Dent soon hit his dramatic home run, and we were able to paint the New York logo. We also learned that stadium manager Johnny Johnson was a wonderful Herk Robinson impersonator.

Don't get me wrong—Herk is a great guy, but he just got on your nerves with little things. When the Royals were winning pennants, we had fun.

I am convinced Herk could have been a world-class groundskeeper if he wanted. One time he called me up and said his Zoysia grass had some brown spots. Luckily, Dr. John Dunn from the University of Missouri was paying me a visit, and Dr. Dunn is one of the best Zoysia men in the nation. We went out there and walked up to the lawn, and John said, "That's the most beautiful grass I've seen." So we walked over the lawn, and there were a few brown spots about the size of a silver dollar. We checked out the lawn, and Dr. Dunn said there was nothing to worry about. Herk said, "It doesn't look good from the bedroom window," but that's Herk, the perfectionist. You have to give him credit for wanting only the best.

I'll tell you how much of a perfectionist Herk is. John Schuerholz was getting married and wanted to have his photo taken in Herk's garden, which is a beautiful backdrop. Herk wanted everything perfect, so he had his wife climb a ladder and pull any unsightly leaves off the trees so they wouldn't show up in the picture. That says a lot about Herk—and about his wife. They want the best, and then some.

Only a couple of people could make Herk laugh—Jack McKeon, the former manager, and Hal McRae. Hal used to get on him and say, "You have your pants on so high. Is a flood coming to town?"

We didn't always see eye to eye, but I loved the guy. If he would have made decisions and operated the ball club like he takes care of his lawn, flowers and trees, the Royals would have been in the World Series every year. It's amazing what he can do with trees, plants, grass and shrubs. He's the world's best. I still love the man, and he had a great father, whom I also admired.

And then there was the run in about the baseball caps. One day I went up to Volume Services, our stadium vendor, and bought two caps, one for me and one for my assistant, Smokey Olsen. After dickering on the price, I got a receipt and walked away.

As soon as I got down to the field, Dean Vogelaar, the public relations director, blew past me like a tornado to where John Schuerholz was seated in the dugout. John said, "Hey George, come over here. I want to talk to you. Where did you get those caps?"

"I just bought them up at Volume Services," I said and showed him the receipt. He told Dean, "These aren't our caps." Dean was trying to get Al Zych, our equipment manager, in trouble for giving away caps.

The next day, I went up to see Dean. I said, "Dean, you and I both work for the Kansas City Royals. But starting today, don't you ever talk to me again. If it's business, I'll give you 100 percent, but if it's not about the Royals, stay the hell away from me, and I'll stay the hell away from you."

Finally, Dean had traveling secretary Bill Beck come tell me he was sorry. Bygones are bygones.

Although I no longer work for the Royals, I wish them nothing but the best. I am convinced David Glass will turn the franchise around. If he can make a big company out of Wal-Mart, he's the kind of guy I'd like to work for—and then some.

Jack Steadman, the former president of the Chiefs, could be as finicky as Herk Robinson, only about his car. He used to warn us not to water the grass and trees near the executive parking lot when his car was there. But when the summer heat blew off the asphalt, we had to water the young grass, or it would die. So I always had a crew member with a Turkish towel on hand to wipe off any water that hit Steadman's car.

One day, I didn't see Jack's car in the lot, so I decided to give the grass a good soaking. Late that afternoon, I got a message to see him in his office the first thing the next morning. Jack said, "What did I tell you about watering the grass and trees?"

I said, "Jack, when I water, I have a man there with a nice soft towel to wipe any water off your car. I looked personally, and your car wasn't there, so I gave it some water."

He said, "No, my car wasn't there—but my wife's convertible Thunderbird was in the next spot with the top down."

I guess there was a good amount of water on the floor of Martha Steadman's Thunderbird. You win some, and you lose some. That's why I never got a raise. I got slapped on the wrist and slashed in the pocketbook. The grass was more important to me than Jack's car.

No discussion of owners would be complete without mentioning Lamar Hunt, the nicest multimillionaire you could ever hope to meet. I was just a poor kid, but Lamar would come down and work and talk with me. All these years later, Lamar still gives my family and me preferred parking and great seats at Arrowhead Stadium.

Not bad, I'd say, considering I threw him off my field in his first visit to Municipal Stadium.

CHAPTER 14

A Kick in the Grass

Although Lamar Hunt is enshrined in the NFL Hall of Fame, his first love has always been soccer. He played collegiately at SMU, and he was a driving force in the old North American Soccer League, which tried to make inroads among sports fans in the United States.

The Kansas City Spurs, with owner John Latshaw and general manager John Tyler, played at Municipal Stadium in the late 1960s and early 1970s. They were one of the more successful franchises in the league. I learned to love soccer, both as a fan and as a groundskeeper. Unlike football, where most of the wear and tear is between the hash marks, damage to soccer fields is random and usually light, except in front of the goal mouth. The Spurs were a nice addition to the A's and Chiefs, giving me a third sport to focus on.

One of the best compliments I have ever received was from the great Brazilian star Pele, who played for the New York Cosmos. Pele told me the field at Municipal Stadium was the second-best pitch he had ever played on, right behind London's Wembley Stadium.

After the NASL folded, I only worked an occasional exhibition game. One Saturday night, the Dallas Tornadoes played a Russian team at Arrowhead Stadium, and the Chiefs were scheduled to play the Minnesota Vikings the next night. After the soccer game, my crew had to scrub the lines off the artificial turf to repaint for the next day.

We finally decided to knock it off around midnight and finish the next morning. During the night, the leftover ammonia solution ate through the brass in the tank,

Can you grow grass on plywood? You sure can, as we proved in this demonstration for the 1994 World Cup selection committee.

and it exploded in my face the next day. If it weren't for the fast action of Bobby Yarborough, the Chiefs equipment manager, and Dr. Rolfe Becker, the team eye doctor, I probably would be blind today. I give them credit for saving my eyesight.

We had a shot at bringing big-time soccer to Arrowhead for the 1994 World Cup in the United States. However, FIFA, the international governing body of soccer, required a natural playing surface and a wider field than we had at Arrowhead.

We got together with HOK Architects, which had designed the stadium, and came up with a plan to install a raised surface into the third or fourth row of seats and basically grow grass on plywood. We had 21 days to prove that our crazy idea would work.

I built a scale model of the field and had about a dozen test plots where we grew grass on geotextile laid on top of

CHAPTER 15

GUTEN TAG AND ALOHA

The spray technician from the golf course in Pasadena sprayed the field for us, but one day I saw a new applicator on the tractor. Before I caught up with him, he had put about four chemicals in the spray tank and started going around the field. The only problem was, he forgot to agitate the spray solution and burned the grass. All we could do at that late date was paint a green border around the field, but it still looked fine for the worldwide television audience.

I had to help out with a similar problem at the 1996 Summer Olympics in Atlanta. Executive director Billy Payne called me at home and said, "George, can you please come down here? The sod has died on the field for the opening ceremonies." I rearranged a trip to Monterrey, Mexico, for an NFL preseason game and caught a plane to Atlanta.

We had just 12 hours to prepare the base and 24 hours to sod Olympic Stadium. We had sod shipped in from Arkansas, and Eddie Woerner from Eddie Woerner Turf Farm came in and laid it. The crew worked around the clock. Valley Quest Landscaping did a great job. I remember sleeping in Chipper Jones's locker in the corner, and being five-foot-four, I fit right in. Another time, I fell asleep in Eddie Mangan's wheelbarrow at 2 a.m. and slept until 6 a.m. Eddie put a fan next to me before going to sleep in the clubhouse. I believe that was the best sleep I ever had. But we pulled it off, and the opening ceremonies came off without a hitch, thanks to Eddie and a great crew.

As I said, it's always fun to try new sports and new events, although I wish it weren't always an emergency situation. The only thing more fun than facing new challenges at home is trying them overseas, which the NFL also gave me the opportunity to do.

plywood. We even had miniature soccer players on the field for the demonstration. But although the test was a great success, FIFA awarded its nearest Midwest location to Soldier Field in Chicago.

Dr. James Watson, my old friend from Toro, was the head agronomist for the World Cup. I assisted him on all nine venues and was in charge of Soldier Field and the Silverdome in Pontiac, Michigan. I remember resodding the field in Chicago. It had to be two inches thick to stand up to all of the people who would be on the field for opening ceremonies, and it did just fine.

The Silverdome was quite another challenge. Besides being artificial turf, it was indoors. Michigan State University agronomists came up with the idea of growing grass on trays in the parking lot, which would be moved into the stadium just in time for the game. The system worked OK, although the grass didn't have much stamina and would not have held up for very many games. Looking back, we probably would have been better off covering the floor of the stadium with a crushed limestone mix and sodding right on top of it.

I always enjoy trying new sports like soccer. Growing grass is growing grass, but every sport has different demands that keep you on your toes. My experiences with the Olympic Games would have been much more enjoyable if I had been in the loop from the beginning instead of always being brought in to put out fires.

In 1984, the grass died at the Rose Bowl in Pasadena about three weeks before the start of the Olympic soccer tournament. In fact, the crew was bringing in dead sod that was painted green. We put down about 200 tons of sand to top-dress it, then pushed it up with urea for three weeks. I went home to Kansas City, then returned just before soccer play began.

For a poor kid from eastern Pennsylvania, I have been fortunate to have had the opportunity to travel throughout the world.

First, Uncle Sam gave me an all-expenses-paid trip to Korea. Then, the NFL gave me the opportunity to work on fields from Tokyo to Mexico City to Barcelona. As proud as I was to serve my country, I think I prefer growing grass to dodging bullets.

The NFL plays one international game each preseason to expose the sport to a worldwide audience. I have prepared the fields for most of these games, as well as the championship field for the World League of American Football, which now is known as NFL Europe.

I once had to convert historic Wembley Stadium in London from soccer to football for the championship game, just as I did at Arrowhead. Germany played England in soccer in a rainstorm on Saturday, and we had to work in the rain to paint "London" in one end zone and "Barcelona" in the other for the title game. Wembley is great for soccer, but when you get those 300-pound linemen hitting out there, it's a different story. But we got it done.

One year in Barcelona, we had to do a lot of reseeding in Olympic Stadium. Even though a water line broke in the middle of the field the day before the game, it turned out fine.

In Mexico City, they grow a grass called kukuyu, and because they cut it the same direction all the time, it has a grain. We needed to roll the field, and a local crew member came up with an old roller that must have been used by

Abe Lincoln—he had to wire the gas pedal to his toe. Because we couldn't get a crane into Azteca Stadium, it took about 50 guys on carpenter scaffolding to put up the goal post nets. Those guys are hard workers down there and a pleasure to work with.

Berlin was one of the most interesting experiences. We had to paint nine football fields on a big practice area outside Olympic Stadium called Maifield, where Benito Mussolini once spoke to more than a million people. They had a Turkish groundskeeper who made people wash their feet before going on the field, and they watered it by hand.

On my first trip to Berlin, I was sitting in the lobby of the InterContinental Hotel when police with dogs swarmed in. I later learned that Secretary of State James Baker was staying there.

The next morning, I got up, went to the NFL office and saw my boss, Jim Steeg. I asked him what needed to be done at Olympic Stadium that day. "We're not going today," he said. "We're going to see them take down Checkpoint Charlie at the Berlin Wall."

I said, "You people go, I have work to do." Eddie Mangan and I went to the stadium. Later on, I sent Eddie to get some rock from the wall. About four years later when we returned to Berlin, my wife said, "You have to see where the Berlin wall was." I'm not a tourist, but I guess I need to take more time to stop and smell the roses (which were only about a 10-minute walk away).

Hawaii has long been one of my favorite places to work. (Maybe it's because there are so many Tomas in the phone book.) The first time I went to prepare Aloha Stadium for the Pro Bowl, I think everyone was expecting a Japanese man, not a Ukrainian. But I hit it off immediately with the Hawaiian people and have gotten along great for more than a quarter-century since.

I had a great crew for the 2000 Pro Bowl at Aloha Stadium. In the back row are Walter Komatsubara, me and my son, Chip. In the front row are Show Ikeda from Japan, Bobby Slavy from the San Diego Chargers and Brian Johnson from the Arizona Cardinals.

As a matter of fact, I would say the best people I have ever worked with in the world have been the crew at Aloha Stadium. They are dedicated to their jobs, and they keep everything nice and neat. I go back every chance I get, and I helped the NFL convert the Astroturf surface to FieldTurf after the 2003 Pro Bowl.

Hawaii is an unusual place to work, though. First, the cost of building new fields is much higher than on the mainland, because everything must be shipped in. Believe it or not, we even have to ship in sand, because the local sand is too fine for soil mixes. Second, because everything grows so fast, we have to mow every day. And unlike the mainland, there is no off season to regroup and repair the field and equipment.

And then there are the ancient religions. Legend has it that Aloha Stadium was built on a burial ground. One year, the crew tried to change the configuration from football to baseball, and the stands wouldn't budge. Experts were brought in from the mainland, but nothing they tried would work.

I got to the stadium early one morning and saw that ti leaves had been spread around the perimeter of the football field as an offering to the gods. Sure enough, the crew was able to move the stands. It made a believer out of me.

One year, I stayed to build two practice fields for University of Hawaii football coach June Jones. I looked at the plans, and they were all wrong. Where was the drainage? Where was the crown? Finally, I asked the designer, "Have you ever walked on a professional field?" He said, "No. I got my information at the library." You have to watch them over there so they don't waste the poor taxpayers' money.

You also have to stipulate details in the contract, such as no stones larger than one-quarter inch in the top foot of the soil. Even so, I saw rocks the size of golf balls. We had a new field in eight weeks, and June got us a new aerifier. After a few passes, it broke to pieces, hitting rocks as big as baseballs. We also broke a $35,000 verti-drain. We had to haul out some of the biggest rocks, which were as big as water coolers, with a high loader.

The quality of the workers dropped off dramatically from Aloha Stadium to the university, but in the end, we wound up with practice fields that would rival any in the

NFL. Between four and six quarterbacks threw in the same place every day, and there was never a bare spot. Now, with Herman Frazier as athletics director and Tom Sadler as his assistant, they will turn it around.

When people build fields wrong, everyone suffers—the taxpayers, the athletes, the coaches and the groundskeepers. Hawaii is not alone, however. A lot of fields that have been built in recent years have fallen apart after the first game or have had to be redone after the season ended. In some cases, they even had to remove the root zone and start from scratch as the Cleveland Browns had to do.

What makes it even worse is that a lot of these people don't want to listen to sound advice. The top groundskeepers can talk until they are blue in the face, but nobody is going to listen. Many of the contractors do a good job, but some do a bad job—and a lot of them keep right on getting hired. If I hired one of them, I would be there every day to make sure they did their jobs. It's heartbreaking to see things like this happen.

I saw the same problems in Maui, where I worked on War Memorial Stadium, the home of the Hula Bowl. They have excellent workers who want to learn, but the department heads just don't care. Their attitude seems to be, "We have gotten by all these years, so why change now?" That explains why they built a beautiful stadium for their women's softball team but then had to spend $350,000 to raise the field because the players could not see home plate. You would think they would want to do a better job for the safety of the kids who play on the field, but many times it seems they don't care.

We had 12 days to prepare the field, which was *really* bad, for the University of Hawaii Warriors' opening game in 2002, which June Jones had moved from Honolulu to

Maui. I rolled the field with an eight-ton roller, aerified it, seeded pregerminated ryegrass and Bermuda and played on it eight days later. The footing for the players was excellent, and the color of the grass was great. Coach Jones gave me the game ball, and the Hawaii Quarterback Club named me the player of the month for August.

Perhaps the most interesting trip I ever took was to Gezer Kibbutz in Israel for 17 days in 1997 to build a baseball field for the Maccabbee Games, which is the international Jewish Olympics.

How did the Nitty Gritty Dirt Man wind up in Israel, of all places? Credit David Leichman, who runs the education center at Gezer Kibbutz, whom I happened to meet when he visited Kansas City.

The field at the kibbutz was being used twice a day for everything from softball to Little League baseball to soccer. The U.S. Embassy, British Embassy and U.S. Marines all played there, along with the Israeli national team. David was worried about the condition of the field, needed help to fix it up for the games, and I agreed to go.

Although the field was in bad shape, the setting was beautiful. Right past the center field wall, you could see Tel-Gezer, the mountain where King Solomon lived. There were a lot of humps and lips on the field, and we took care of them first. I used sand to try to improve the dirt. Some red dirt is available in Israel, but it's expensive, and you have to haul it a long way.

The turf itself, Bermuda grass with some rye mixed in, was in reasonably good condition. There is little disease pressure in the desert, but weeds are a problem. Fertilizer was another problem. Fertilizer in Israel is made for liquid application. It's damp and fine like sugar, not in pellets as it is here. You may apply 20-20-20, for example, but that may not be what you actually get. I did the best I could with what I had to work with and also applied potash, phosphorous and ammonium sulfate separately. While waiting for the grass to grow, I built a pitching mound and separate bullpens for baseball and softball.

Water is the lifeblood of a kibbutz, and Israelis have mastered the art and science of water-conserving drip irrigation. The entire outfield was irrigated, and I used the fire hose at the kibbutz to water the infield.

I can't say enough about my "crew." I loved the way everyone at the kibbutz pitched in and worked together in the glue factory and growing corn. Everyone also ate breakfast, lunch and dinner together.

Building that baseball field reminded me of Edwardsville because of all of the rocks. The preschoolers picked up the small ones, while the grade school kids helped out with the larger ones. They were great people, and they loved baseball. There were a couple of 14- and 15-year-olds who could become good groundskeepers with the proper training.

Unlike my trip to Germany, I decided to sample the local culture. I was at the kibbutz for Passover and got to share in a wonderful meal. Some Arab families in the community also invited us to share one of their holidays. Although their home was made of mud concrete, it was very clean inside. They sacrificed a lamb and served it over pita bread and rice on a large platter. Everyone sat, ate with their hands and talked. I had never seen so much food. I usually am not a lamb eater, but I couldn't stop eating it that day.

After everybody was finished, they passed around a water pipe with apple tobacco. I was watching everybody and thought, "What do I know about a water pipe? I'm just a groundskeeper." When it came to me, instead of sucking it in, I blew into it, like Lawrence Welk blowing bubbles. That liquid went all over the place. Oh, did they laugh. And then they had a big party before I left, and the Arabs gave me a water pipe to bring home.

Now, I'm a groundskeeper, not a diplomat, but seeing the Jews and Arabs get along in that part of Israel gives me great hope for world peace. In fact, if everyone had the opportunities to experience other cultures as I have, we might all get along a little better.

CHAPTER 16

TOMA TO THE RESCUE

After the Gulf War in 1991, the legendary Red Adair was brought to Kuwait to put out the oil wells that Saddam Hussein's troops had set ablaze. Sometimes, I feel like the Red Adair of groundskeeping, being brought in to solve a crisis.

Why are there so many problems? I can give you three reasons: Some bad contractors, bad agronomists and bad groundskeepers.

Take the new football stadium in Cleveland. The field fell apart during the first game that the Browns played, and they had to rip out the root zone mix and start from scratch as soon as the season ended. With all of today's technology, why? Contractors have to start doing a better job.

When the Chiefs held training camp at William Jewell College in Liberty, Missouri, we built a practice field for $25,000 that was better than some $1 million fields today, especially the tray system they use in the Meadowlands. How could it have stood up to all of the events that were held on it while the Meadowlands has to be sodded twice in a week? Somewhere, somebody fell asleep—and now they have converted to FieldTurf.

Some of today's agronomists and groundskeepers are the best advertising for artificial turf. We need to step it up a notch, or a lot of these stadiums will be switching to FieldTurf or one of the 28 other new playing surfaces now on the market. To be honest, there are better fields in high schools, colleges and the minor leagues than in some professional stadiums. As Alan Sigwart of Miami, one of the top groundskeepers, told me, we must do a better job, or we will be out of our jobs. Artificial FieldTurf will take over—and let me tell you, it is. In my part of the country alone, the University of Missouri and Kansas State University have gone to FieldTurf, and the University of Kansas is playing on Astro Play.

The announcers ripped the Tennessee Titans' field during a *Monday Night Football* game in the 2002 season. The first reaction is always to blame the groundskeeper. In this case, he happened to be Terry Porch, who started working for me when he was only 16 years old. Sometimes, we need to look around at the contractors and sod suppliers before fixing the blame. I called Terry after that game to encourage him. He had done the best job he could with what he had to work with.

We need to be prepared. Dan LeBlanc, a 45-year-old former truck driver and now full-time groundskeeper, has turned Holman Stadium in Nashua, New Hampshire, into a showplace. Why can it be done in the minor leagues but not at the highest levels of play?

Other times, however, the problems are not the fault of a contractor, agronomist or groundskeeper, but Mother Nature. That certainly was the case when I got called in to help prepare Candlestick Park for the playoffs during torrential downpours in northern California.

The first priority in this type of situation is player safety. As Hank Stram said, you can play football on a pillow of marshmallows, and somebody is going to get hurt. As a groundskeeper, you have to prevent injuries or people will just look at us as another guy cutting grass. The cheapest insurance for an athlete is a safe playing field.

The grounds crew at Candlestick pumped the water out, then we put in sand and leveled off the field, and West Coast Turf sodded it from hash mark to hash mark. After the game, there were only two divots. We could have played a triple-header, thanks to Barry Mohon of West Coast Turf.

Dianne Feinstein, who was mayor of San Francisco at the time, took charge like General George Patton. She was down there in the mud with the rest of us, and I'll never forget her great attitude. We need more people like her in this game.

The next time I had to go to Candlestick, it was harder to get the crew motivated. There were a lot of things wrong and not much time to work on them. Putting the field back in shape was easy; the hard thing was being a coach for the guys on the crew. The old crew had it, but the new crew seemed to have lost it—big time.

Fog, not rain, was the problem for a championship game between Mike Ditka's Bears and Buddy Ryan's Eagles at Soldier Field in Chicago. I stood in the end zone and couldn't see the 10-yard line. Ditka told me, "George, you thawed the field so good and the ground is so hot that it caused the fog." That was a memorable game.

I was called on to help with Soldier Field another time after the Bears had installed Prescription Athletic Turf, or PAT. It seems there were troubles every place that PAT had been installed. After the first game, it fell apart. Coach Don Shula of the Miami Dolphins, their next opponent, called me to see if they could get their game moved to another field. I said, "Coach, I'm just the Nitty Gritty Dirt Man. Go talk to the league." But we were able to sod the center of the field, and it worked fine. When we got back to Kansas City, the McCloskey family had sent us a large television set to show their appreciation.

I also love helping out on college fields, because I always learn a few things that I can bring to the NFL games. One year, I got a call on the Saturday before Christmas

I have worked at dozens of NFL and college football stadiums, and Soldier Field in Chicago has long been one of my favorites.

from officials at the Senior Bowl in Mobile, Alabama, saying they were having problems with their grass. I flew down and helped them get started resodding.

When I got back home on Tuesday, I got a call from the people at the Superdome in New Orleans, who were getting ready for the Sugar Bowl game between Florida State and Virginia Tech. Seminole coach Bobby Bowden is one of my favorite people, so I went down to help. That's where we came up with the idea of the "Toma Line," a dark eight-inch line between the white border and the hash marks. It helps officials on close plays after players wipe out the white border with their cleats. I think it's a great idea and would like to see the NFL adopt it. It keeps the line markings on the money.

I also have had to bail out a few baseball fields over the years. Jim Fregosi once had me come to Philadelphia to build a pitching mound for the Phillies. Veterans Stadium has always been a bad field, with dirty Astroturf that is poorly maintained. The pitchers were happy with the new mound, and the team even sent their grounds crew to Kansas City to see how we did things.

Then in 2000, I was asked to come salvage Hammond Stadium in Fort Myers, Florida, just eight days before the Florida State League All-Star game. Nematodes, which are microscopic worms that live in the soil, had chewed up the roots of the grass.

We had to remove all of the infield grass to a depth of eight inches, then take out another four inches of soil, from foul pole to foul pole and about 45 feet back into the outfield. We filled it back in with a mixture of 70 percent sand and 30 percent peat moss. After laser-grading the field, we used every fire hose we could find to flood the field and settle the sand.

Even though it was dry in Fort Myers, it was raining a half-hour away in Punta Gorda, Florida, the nearest location of Eddie Woerner's Turf Farm. We decided to get sod instead from his farm in Tifton, Georgia, but a hurricane rolled through as soon as the crew had cut the first load. So we went back and cut 30-inch rolls of saturated sod at Punta Gorda. It came out beautifully. Ed Woerner has the best sod grown on plastic that I have ever seen. He is simply the best at this.

In the end, we had a new field in just eight days. The players raved about it, and it was selected field of the year for the league. The crew received well-deserved accolades and a wonderful letter from the president of the Florida State League. I have been invited back every year since to work spring training on the field for the Minnesota Twins.

Rescue jobs may look nice on the resume after the fact, but they can be a little stressful at the time. I'd much rather be in on a project to prevent problems before they start. As the old saying goes, "The impossible we can do immediately. The miraculous takes a little longer."

CHAPTER 17

FAKE GRASS, REAL CHALLENGES

People who don't know me often think they can get a rise out of me by mentioning those dreaded words: "artificial turf." But the simple reality is, I only have a strong dislike for bad installations or poorly maintained artificial turf.

There are good and bad artificial surfaces, just as there is good and bad grass. And in most cases, the only difference between good and bad is the people who install and maintain them.

One of the biggest misconceptions about groundskeeping is that it is easier to maintain an artificial field than a natural one. After all, vacuuming your living room is easier than mowing your lawn. But if anything, artificial turf is more difficult—at least if it's done right. When Arrowhead Stadium had artificial turf, it took four men three days to clean it after a 60-minute game—that's 96 man hours. By contrast, it took only 10 hours a week to maintain the Chiefs' grass practice field, which was used four or five days a week.

FieldTurf and other modern surfaces are light years ahead of the original Astroturf, which was invented by the same genius who decided to play baseball and football indoors. I remember when a game between the Houston Oilers and San Diego Chargers had to be cancelled because the field was so bad.

The crew at the Astrodome used to cover the baseball infield with one large roll of Astroturf for football. After the game, it went back onto a large reel and was stored beneath the floor. The problem was, they never smoothed the base pits, and the wood around them was rotten. When the carpet went down, it was like craters on the moon, and players could have gotten injured. Player safety must be our top priority.

I mentioned earlier how poor the original Tartan Turf field was at Royals Stadium. The team soon converted to drain-through Astroturf with an asphalt base. Of course, the contractors managed to mess up the base. I would stand in the home bullpen, roll a baseball toward home plate, and it would be just like a washboard.

I have never hesitated to voice my opinion. But Herk Robinson told George Humphries and me to lay off the Astroturf people and the contractor, so we did. A couple of days later, I got a call from John Schuerholz to meet him and Dean Vogelaar on the field. John walked the infield and found some large holes in the asphalt. He marked some of them with a set of car keys. He wanted them fixed. The grounds crew wrote a letter to Herk saying how bad the installation was. But Herk and Joe Burke did not care. I still have the letter.

Who suffers? The players, the grounds crew and most of all, the taxpayers. Now the Royals and Chiefs are asking for a special bi-state tax in Missouri and Kansas to upgrade the stadiums. I would vote for it today, but first they have to show me how the money would be spent, as well as who will be in charge of the project.

Who will oversee the construction, and how will they do it? Why should taxpayers put their money into the stadium if slipshod work is acceptable? Wasting the taxpayers' hard-earned money doesn't make much sense. I believe we owe it to them to work as if it were our own money we were spending.

I knew what to look for when the Chiefs installed OmniTurf in their practice facility. My son, Chip, was head groundskeeper, and I was the consultant. I was tough on the contractors from day one. Chip and I stretched string across the field and marked all of the dips deeper than 1/4 inch with fluorescent paint. I told the county not to accept the work and this time, they listened.

The OmniTurf people argued about their installation, saying they would bring in experts from Germany to look at the field. They did, and about 15 minutes into our meeting, they said, "George is right. Pay up." I have many friends in the artificial turf business, so I know the tricks of the trade. You can't beat people such as Jim Seigle, Walt Schonke and Bud Garner of Astroturf and Pierre Alarie of FieldTurf. One time, Walt "The Smiling Hawaiian" Schonke was working for OmniTurf, and I was consulting for the Royals in Florida. The installation was bad, and Walt flew all the way from St. Louis to Honolulu to apologize to me in person.

The thing to keep in mind is that artificial turf doesn't take care of itself. At the Super Bowl in the Metrodome in Minneapolis, we painted the entire field green, because the carpet wasn't green enough to suit television. We did the same thing again at the Superdome so it would look good on television.

My good friend Rush Limbaugh mentioned on his radio show how we got on our hands and knees to get the lint off the field and seal every seam with hot glue. We even used to go to fields at night and shine headlights across them to check for evenness. Again, player safety must come first.

Several installers have made their mark in the profession with their expertise in artificial turf. Bud Gardner was one of the best ever on Astroturf. Bud is retired now and living in Hilo, Hawaii. Pierre Alarie is my choice for rubber-based surfaces such as AstroPlay and FieldTurf. Pierre and Bud could do it all.

Where is the profession headed? Back in the 1960s and 1970s, artificial turf was all the rage. Then the pendulum swung back toward natural grass to protect high-priced ballplayers. Now, the trend is toward the new generation of artificial surfaces, such as FieldTurf, AstroPlay, Sportexe, ProGreen and many others that are on the market today. But just as with natural grass, it all starts with a good installation.

People who work for artificial turf companies cringe to this day when they hear the name George Toma. But you know what? I don't work for them. I work for the players, the owners and the taxpayers who fund the stadiums.

CHAPTER 18

THE END OF GRASS?

Although it may not make the *New York Times* bestseller lists, the National Football League Players Association's annual survey of playing surfaces is fascinating reading for those of us in the business.

The survey released in January 2003 was a stunner. Players ranked the new FieldTurf surface in Seahawks Stadium in Seattle as third best in the league—and ahead of 20 natural grass fields. Only the natural-grass fields in Tampa Bay and Arizona were ranked higher. I often have joked that poor groundskeeping is the best advertising for artificial turf, but it's no longer funny for those of us who are passionate about natural grass.

Here are the top five fields: Tampa Bay, Arizona, Seattle, Carolina and Jacksonville. The bottom five are Philadelphia, the Meadowlands, Cincinnati, Minnesota and New Orleans. One of those, the Meadowlands, was replaced before the start of the 2003 season.

What is most disturbing to me is that this was the first time ever that five of the 10 worst fields were natural grass. As Gene Upshaw, executive director of the Players Association noted, players have a strong preference for playing on grass, but this alone is no longer a guarantee of an excellent field.

Don't get me wrong—I have nothing against artificial surfaces. I spent a great deal of my career with the Kansas City Chiefs and Royals taking care of the ones in the Truman Sports Complex. I certainly understand the many advantages of FieldTurf and other new generation surfaces. However, it bothers me that the reason many teams are converting their fields is because others in my profession are not doing their jobs.

The other interesting statistic is that 90 percent of NFL players say they prefer to play on grass. Reading between the lines, I would say that while they may like grass, they prefer a good artificial surface to a bad natural one like the Meadowlands used to be, when quarterback Kerry Collins referred to it as "borderline dangerous." Every artificial surface that has been replaced with natural grass had to be redone. Every one of them.

FieldTurf is simply the right product at the right time. I'll never forget the first time I saw it down at Georgia Tech University. Now remember, I have been maintaining grass for six decades, but the first time I saw FieldTurf, I honestly thought it was natural grass. I had to go back and look at it a second time. It looks like grass, it feels like grass and most importantly, it plays like grass.

The FieldTurf concept is simple—synthetic turf should be like grass, not carpet. FieldTurf's inventors were sports people, not carpet makers. They were former players and coaches, not turf salesmen. They approached the challenge from a completely different perspective. They wanted to develop a synthetic system that combined the benefits of natural grass with the best attributes of a durable synthetic system: all-weather playability, low maintenance and unlimited playing time.

FieldTurf is dramatically different from traditional synthetic turf. The most striking difference is immediately obvious. Instead of a dense, abrasive rug, FieldTurf's fiber surface feels like new blades of grass. Rug burns are a thing of the past. Unlike traditional artificial turf, FieldTurf does not rely on an underlying shock pad for safety, resilience and player comfort. Rather, like its natural grass cousin,

FieldTurf's grass fibers are surrounded and stabilized by a special blend of smooth, rounded silica sand, rubber granules and "Nike Grind," made of ground-up athletic shoe material. The result? A stable, resilient, uniform, shock-absorbing surface.

Developers spent years to bring FieldTurf to the market, using it for tennis and golf, then soccer, and then they finally perfected it for football and baseball. The University of Nebraska was the first Division I football program to install it in 1999. Since then, 60 Division I teams have switched to FieldTurf, including two from my part of the country, Kansas State University and the University of Missouri. The Seattle Seahawks and Detroit Lions installed FieldTurf in their new stadiums, and the Meadowlands (finally) and the Georgia Dome converted to it for the 2003 season. New Orleans' Superdome installed AstroPlay.

I had the opportunity to supervise one of the most challenging FieldTurf installations ever undertaken. It's one of those odds facts that Aloha Stadium, in one of the lushest parts of the world, has always had artificial turf. There are several reasons for that. Hawaii has notoriously poor drainage, the field must stand up to numerous professional, college and high school contests, and the stadium must be reconfigured regularly to accommodate baseball as well as football.

Several years ago, the NFL extended its contract to keep the Pro Bowl in Aloha Stadium. In the contract, the NFL stipulated that it wanted natural grass or another approved playing surface. June Jones, head coach of the University of Hawaii Warriors, had his own ideas. He blamed several injuries to his players on the old Astroturf field. Gary Crowton, head coach at Brigham Young University, also said several of his players were injured on the surface when the two teams played in 2002.

The university and the NFL compromised on FieldTurf.

I began working on the project soon after the Super Bowl in January 2003, and it occupied most of my spring and summer. No one had ever done an installation like this, which required working around pitching mounds, base paths and retractable stands.

And, as always, there were the politics. Taxpayers in Hawaii who had paid $2.4 million for the existing Astroturf surface understandably were not enthusiastic about ripping out a carpet that still had four years left on its warranty.

The FieldTurf cost $1.3 million to install, with the cost split between the state of Hawaii and the NFL. Retaining the Pro Bowl each year will generate more than enough revenue to enable the state to recoup its investment, but there is no way to put a price tag on preventing injuries to young athletes. The cheapest insurance for any athlete is a good, safe playing field. It's money well spent.

It's hard to describe the magnitude of this project. Just consider that we had to bring in about 450 tons of sand from China. We couldn't have done it without having Pierre Alarie on the crew. He designed movable trays, cut rubber geotile mats and worked with drainage and glue to make it all fit together perfectly. Pierre is a perfectionist, which is just what the job demanded.

How is the field performing? It always takes a while to work out the bugs and see how a field plays under a range of conditions. I am interested to see how well it drains during one of the downpours that hit the islands every so often. Heat could be another challenge. The "grass blades" retain a lot of heat, but they can be watered down and cooled off well before the game. I'll tell you one thing—it will never be anything like the blast furnace of the old field at Kauffman Stadium.

I do not endorse any of the sand-rubber artificial turf infills. There are a few dozen on the market today—take your pick. Study them all before you decide, and don't talk to the front office. Talk to the groundskeeper if he doesn't operate under the gag rule.

Ultimately, only the players can determine how the field is performing. I told June Jones that his team should be much faster, because they don't need to wear all of that protective gear. If the Warriors don't have a 1,000-yard rusher, I don't know what else we can do to help them.

Even a guy like me, who thinks about turf 365 days a year, has a hard time remembering what team is playing on which surfaces. For the record, these were the fields as of the 2003 season.

Team	*Stadium*	*Playing Surface*
Arizona Cardinals	Sun Devil Stadium	Grass
Atlanta Falcons	Georgia Dome	FieldTurf
Baltimore Ravens	M&T Bank Stadium	Momentum Turf
Buffalo Bills	Ralph Wilson Stadium	AstroPlay
Carolina Panthers	Ericsson Stadium	Grass
Chicago Bears	Soldier Field	Grass
Cincinnati Bengals	Paul Brown Stadium	Grass (heated)
Cleveland Browns	Browns Stadium	Grass (heated)
Dallas Cowboys	Texas Stadium	Texas Turf
Denver Broncos	Invesco Field at Mile High	Grass
Detroit Lions	Ford Field	FieldTurf
Green Bay Packers	Lambeau Field	Grass
Houston Texans	Reliant Stadium	Grass
Indianapolis Colts	RCA Dome	Artificial
Jacksonville Jaguars	Alltel Stadium	Grass
Kansas City Chiefs	Arrowhead Stadium	Grass
Miami Dolphins	Pro Player Stadium	Grass

Minnesota Vikings	Metrodome	Artificial
New England Patriots	Gillette Stadium	Grass
New Orleans Saints	Louisiana Superdome	AstroPlay
New York Giants	Giants Stadium	FieldTurf
New York Jets	Giants Stadium	FieldTurf
Oakland Raiders	Network Associates Coliseum	Grass
Philadelphia Eagles	Lincoln Financial Field	Grass
Pittsburgh Steelers	Heinz Field	Grass
San Diego Chargers	Qualcomm Stadium	Grass
Seattle Seahawks	Seahawks Stadium	FieldTurf
Tampa Bay Buccaneers	Raymond James Stadium	Grass
Tennessee Titans	The Coliseum	Grass
Washington Redskins	FedEx Field	Grass (heated)

Marv Levy, former head coach of the Chiefs and Bills, used to say that football is meant to be played outdoors in the daytime on real grass, and I tend to agree. But if I were a betting man, I would put money on more of those stadiums converting to FieldTurf or other sand-rubber infills in the near future.

Natural grass remains the surface of choice in Major League Baseball, but again, we must do a much better job of maintaining both the grass and the all-important dirt. Here is what teams were playing on in 2003:

Team	*Stadium*	*Playing Surface*
Anaheim Angels	Edison International	Grass
Arizona Diamondbacks	Bank One Ballpark	Grass
Atlanta Braves	Turner Field	Grass
Baltimore Orioles	Camden Yards	Grass
Boston Red Sox	Fenway Park	Grass
Chicago Cubs	Wrigley Field	Grass

Chicago White Sox	U.S Cellular Field	Grass
Cincinnati Reds	Great American Ball Park	Grass
Cleveland Indians	Jacobs Field	Grass
Colorado Rockies	Coors Field	Grass
Detroit Tigers	Comerica Park	Grass
Florida Marlins	Pro Player Stadium	Grass
Houston Astros	Astros Field	Grass
Kansas City Royals	Kauffman Stadium	Grass
Los Angles Dodgers	Dodger Stadium	Grass
Milwaukee Brewers	Miller Park	Grass
Minnesota Twins	Metrodome	Artificial turf
Montreal Expos	Olympic Stadium	Artificial turf
New York Mets	Shea Stadium	Grass
New York Yankees	Yankee Stadium	Grass
Oakland A's	Network Associates Coliseum	Grass
Philadelphia Phillies	Veterans Stadium	Artificial turf
Pittsburgh Pirates	PNC Park	Grass
St. Louis Cardinals	Busch Stadium	Grass
San Diego Padres	Qualcomm Stadium	Grass
San Francisco Giants	Pacific Bell Park	Grass
Seattle Mariners	Safeco Field	Grass
Tampa Bay Devil Rays	Tropicana Field	FieldTurf
Texas Rangers	Ballpark in Arlington	Grass
Toronto Blue Jays	SkyDome	Artificial turf

I may be old fashioned, but I believe the smell of newly mowed grass is as much a part of the baseball experience as eating a hot dog and hearing the crack of the bat. I can't help thinking what my old boss, Charlie O. Finley, would think of the new surfaces. I can see him now, having me apply perfume to make it smell like real grass.

You know me—I'm a grass-and-dirt man from way back. But I'll tell you this: We need to grow grass better.

And if you can't grow grass, you need to go with one of the sand/rubber infills on the market today. Again, I do not endorse any of them, but person to person I will tell you the top five.

CHAPTER 19

THE STATE OF THE ART

Without a doubt, professional groundskeeping today has become far more sophisticated than I could have dreamed when I started out at Artillery Park.

Now we have more money, better equipment, more varieties of grass and pesticides to treat every problem you can imagine. Colleges now make grounds management part of their horticultural programs. Experts with advanced degrees in agronomy can answer nearly any question.

Yes, we are more sophisticated—but are we better? I would argue that we may have become too sophisticated for our own good. Emil Bossard had few of the modern amenities we take for granted, but I have yet to meet the groundskeeper who can hold a candle to him. Then you look at the Meadowlands in New Jersey. They spent nearly three million dollars on that field in just three years and still couldn't get it right. If you can't do the job on grass, that's the cheapest advertising there is for artificial turf. And it is—the stadium now has been converted to FieldTurf.

That's a shame, because I often have told Jim Steeg, my boss with the NFL, that I could go in there and grow grass, even using the tray system. During the last two weeks of the 2002 playoffs, they sodded twice, at a cost of $240,000, and still put the wrong sod in. We need to go back to the old ways of doing things.

The Meadowlands, of course, usually is at the top of the list of bad fields as rated by NFL players. I agree that the rankings can be helpful in lighting a fire under groundskeepers, but they also can be somewhat misleading.

For example, one dual-purpose field has to convert between baseball and football early in the season, and the football players who come in during that time give it low marks. But as soon as baseball season ends, it becomes a beautiful field for football. Players may rank, say, Miami or Oakland, low, because they remember playing on the infield dirt, but once they sod a baseball infield, they have an excellent field. Some of those fields are rated low, but I believe they are better than some that make the top 10. Maybe the solution is to have players rank the fields a couple of times during the season instead of only once.

By the way, I am convinced we could solve that problem by sodding the infield for football, then taking up the sod to play baseball. I know it can be done with the technology we have today, using the wonderful sod grown on plastic by Eddie Woerner. Eddie cuts that sod 7 feet wide and 41 feet long, and each piece weighs 4,000 pounds. I have seen him sod almost wall to wall in the Louisiana Superdome in just 13 hours, then take it back up in less than eight hours. We could put that grass on the infield a couple of days before a football game and take it up as soon as the game is over. That certainly would solve a lot of problems.

Some field rankings just don't make sense. Why is the FieldTurf that the Seattle Seahawks play on ranked No. 3 in the league while the Detroit Lions' field—built the same year with the same surface—ranked No. 10? Is the maintenance in Detroit really that bad or was there poor FieldTurf installation? If they were installed at the same time, they should rank the same. I encourage the Players Association to take a look at the way they do their rankings, because a lot of people's livelihoods and reputations are on the line.

Or look at all of the money that was wasted experimenting with Zoysia at Bank One Ballpark in Phoenix.

That already had been tried without success just down the road at Sun Devil Stadium in Tempe. If it didn't work in the full sunlight, how in the world were they going to make it work under a retractable roof? The money was wasted.

By now, you know I am not afraid to call a spade a spade. All of us can do a better job, beginning with the architects. Many of the new stadiums built over the past decade are beautifully designed and cater to the fan's every need. But all too often, the playing surface was an afterthought instead of the central focus. Many architects have no concept of what it takes to play the game and create a design that fails to take into account such important things as grade and drainage. If the original field design is bad, how can the groundskeeper do his job?

How bad is it? Even Melissa Stark, the former sideline reporter on *Monday Night Football*, called me during the 2002 season to ask what was wrong with all of the fields. It's getting out of hand.

Then there are the agronomists. Don't get me wrong—there are a lot of wonderful ones out there, starting with my mentor, Dr. James R. Watson. But while they do a wonderful job of instructing their students in the classroom, they often throw everything out the window when called in to consult on a project for a contractor.

I used to think one agronomist, whom I won't name, was going to be the next Dr. James R. Watson. He went to work for a contractor and told me, "This guy should stop building playing fields and start building McDonald's." But when we held a meeting to discuss the project, he didn't say a word, because he was getting paid by the contractor and wanted to keep on being paid. And so, you guessed it, the taxpayers suffered. The grounds crew and players suffered.

Again, there are fine agronomists out there who do things the right way. But there also are too many agronomists who are laughing all the way to the bank. However, the laugh may be on them when more and more stadiums convert to artificial turf and put them out of their jobs.

I suppose I should say a word or two about unions, which are a big part of our business—sometimes for the better and sometimes for the worst. Watching my father and uncles work in the coal mines growing up gave me a strong appreciation for the working men and women of America. Having said that, union rules can drive you nuts at times, especially when you are racing the clock.

One time at the Meadowlands, we had to wait hours to get a few concrete blocks to hold something down on the artificial turf, because there was only one union forklift operator and nobody else could touch the forklift, so valuable time was wasted. Another time, a worker in the Orange Bowl was mowing the grass in the end zone—just 10 feet from being done—when the horn blew and he stopped. Rules are rules, but that put us behind schedule on irrigating and painting. Even the maintenance crew at Kauffman Stadium used to take the long way around the warning track on the way to work but then cut across the field when it was time for lunch or quitting time. That's just the way it goes, I suppose. I have seen very tough unions, like at Chicago's Soldier Field. But in a crisis they all worked together as a well-oiled machine to do the job and then some for the safety of the players, for the fans and for the taxpayers. That is why Soldier Field is one of my favorite stadiums, thanks to Jim Dugan and John Nolan.

The key to successful groundskeeping has nothing to do with grass seed, lawnmowers or fungicides. It has everything to do with the people behind it. There are some excellent groundskeepers in the NFL and Major League Baseball today, and more are honing their skills in the minor leagues and colleges. But there are others who should try different professions, such as selling insurance.

In my opinion, there are two kinds of people in our business—caretakers and groundskeepers. The caretakers do the minimum amount of work to get by, knowing their owners will pay to resod the field throughout the season. Groundskeepers, by contrast, maintain their fields as if re-sodding simply is not an option. Take Dennis Brolin of the New England Patriots. In old Foxboro Stadium, he once had 10 football games, Major League Soccer, international soccer and nine rock concerts in the same year—all without resodding. And that's even with the harsh New England winter. That's what you call a groundskeeper.

Don't get me wrong—I'm not one of those guys who believes everything was better in the old days. I have the opportunity to be around the best of the best almost on a daily basis. I consider these people who are currently in the game or who recently retired to be true groundskeepers.

Dan LeBlanc, Nashua, New Hampshire. Dan just may be the best combination truck driver and groundskeeper in the history of the game.

In the late 1990s, while I was working spring training for the Royals in Baseball City, Florida, the owner of the Nashua Pride baseball team called to offer me a six-month contract to get Holman Field into shape. I flew up there to look at the field, and it was bad. I said, "There's not much time. We have to shut this field down for a week or two to get it ready for opening the Atlantic League baseball season." That wasn't an option because of high school baseball, but we turned it around all the same.

Dan took a special interest in that field and was determined to do whatever it took to make it play and look its best. Dan the Man did it all, and we made a groundskeeper out of him. Football and baseball fans came out of the stands to help with the field. We even had an insurance salesman, John Parolin, drag the infield. Today, I never go to a Super Bowl without Dan being part of my crew.

Pat Sandarone, Baltimore (retired). I knew Pat from way back when he and I were together in the Eastern League in the 1940s and 1950s. He and his father worked for the team in Elmira, New York. Pat, Orioles' manager Earl Weaver, and I used to have contests to see who could grow the best tomatoes. Sandarone knew how to grow grass and tomatoes, and he made the best wine there ever was. Any time the Orioles played in California, they made sure to bring back a load of grapes for Pat.

Don Follett, Washington. If I were picking the best all-around football groundskeeper for grass or artificial turf, I would have to take Don. He can do it all, and he's a tireless worker. Don's a mechanic, he's a painter, he's a carpenter. When he puts up a goal post, you know it's going to be exactly 10 feet above the level of the field.

Don starts at full speed in the morning and at quitting time, he's still going full speed. He is always there on time and is always dedicated to his job. I can't say enough about this man. If I have to go to war on a football field, I sure want Don at my side.

Dick Erickson, Minnesota (retired). Just look at what he had to go through with baseball, soccer and football. He fought all of that snow and ice in the winter and rarely had to resod. Now teams routinely resod three to five times a year.

Steve Wightman, San Diego. Steve does a hell of a job. He has to move the stands with heavy forklifts to convert from baseball to football, but his field always looks great.

Unlike many two-sport stadiums, Qualcomm doesn't have a track with rails to move the seats when switching sports. Instead, Steve has to bring in an eight- or 10-ton forklift to move the seats around the lower deck, and some of those stands can weigh as much as 40 tons.

I always look forward to working with Steve and his crew when the Super Bowl returns to San Diego, as it did in 2003. You have to take your hat off to them. Steve is also lucky to have a great stadium manager in Bill Wilson.

Scotty Parker, St. Louis Rams. Steve Ortmeyer, the general manager of the Rams, called after the team moved from Los Angeles and asked if I would consult for the team and help build a practice field. At the time, they didn't have any property in St. Louis, so we built two practice fields on the Boys Club's property. We got some sorry-looking sod from Oklahoma, but with a little water and fertilizer, it came out fine.

The next challenge was to find an up-and-coming groundskeeper to take over the field. I recommended Scotty Parker, a St. Louis native who then was working on the crew at Joe Robbie Stadium in Miami. Scotty got the job, and he did a good job on the Boys Club fields. Scotty went on to care for the fields at the Rams' new practice facility, as well as the artificial surface at the Edward Jones Dome.

After the Rams started winning, I began to kid Scotty. I said, "I got you the job, and you're not a groundskeeper any more. When I turn on the TV, I see you behind coach Mike Martz with a headset on, and the camera is on you. Everybody thinks you're a coach." Before the game, he even helps warm up the quarterback.

But Scotty does a great job, and I was happy to see him get a Super Bowl ring. If anyone deserves it, Scotty does.

Mark Razum, Colorado. What a job he did in Phoenix for the Oakland A's spring training. He went to Oakland and made that one of the best fields. Then he went to the Colorado Rockies and made it one of the best fields in the league, even after a bad installation. You have to give Mark credit. He has the "and then some."

Eddie Mangan, Atlanta. John Schuerholz, general manager of the Braves, called me for a recommendation for a groundskeeper for Atlanta-Fulton County Stadium. I said, "I have one in mind—Eddie Mangan at Baseball City. I think he will do a good job, because he's so dedicated."

Eddie took the job, and he turned the field around the first year. He's a hard, meticulous worker. Hours mean nothing to Eddie. He is one of the top groundskeepers in professional baseball for single-sport stadiums and is the head groundskeeper for the Super Bowl.

Wade Boggs got hit in the jaw by a bad hop right after the Braves opened Turner Field. I called Eddie and said, "Get ready. There's a big box of shin guards, chest protectors and helmets coming your way for all of the infielders so they don't get killed on your highway infield." But Eddie's tough, and the players and manager like his toughness. If you want to get something done right, get Eddie to do it. I always want him beside me on a baseball or football field.

Simply put, Eddie does it all—the infield, the pitching mound, home plate, the warning track and the edging. His field looks like it was shaved around the edges every day with a straight razor. If I have go to war on a baseball field, I have to take Eddie Mangan, the best, and then some.

Allen Sigwart, Miami. Allen would be the first guy I would hire for a multisport field and he has the best—just look on TV for the best football and baseball field. He does it all—baseball, football, soccer and concerts—in an area with 90 inches of rain a year. When ballplayers say he has a good infield, you know he's a good groundskeeper. If you don't have good dirt, you don't have a field.

Joe Mooney, Boston (retired). Joe was an old Pennsylvania guy from about 18 miles up the road from me in Scranton. I was groundskeeper in Wilkes-Barre when Joe started with the Red Sox. Joe was a tough Irishman, but everybody loved him, even old Tom Yawkey. He was Tom's boy.

David Mellor. David is the best at mowing patterns in the grass.

Roger Bossard, Chicago White Sox, and Barney Lopas, Anaheim. Roger has the best infield in baseball. Roger is on top of the groundskeeping list. He can do it all. The Bossard family is the best name in groundskeeping. Barney has the best outfield.

Trevor Vance, Kansas City Royals. Trevor began working on my tarp crew in the championship season of 1985. He worked his way up through groundskeeping at the sports complex to stadium maintenance and always was part of my Super Bowl crew.

When I retired from the Royals, I encouraged Trevor to apply for my job. I told him I would stay on for three years to train him on natural grass. He has come a long way—I could write a book about Trevor. You soon will hear the name Trevor Vance mentioned among the best in the business. Trevor had the fifth best playing field in the 2003 baseball season. I am very proud of Trevor—he has the "and then some."

Scott Martin, Kansas City Chiefs. I found Scotty sweeping the stands after Royals games when he was in high school. Now he is an assistant to Andre Bruce of the Chiefs. I want him and Doug Schallenberg of the Chiefs on my side.

John Cundiff, Kansas City. John followed me around the field like he was a magnet and I was metal, soaking up information. The Weed Man now runs Turf's Up, one of the top 10 new lawn companies in the nation.

P.J. Boutwell, Fort Myers, Florida. P.J., who prepares Hammond Field for the Florida State League and the Minnesota Twins' spring training, may well be the next Eddie Mangan. He does it all, from irrigation to mechanics to mower patterns to dirt infields. You will be hearing his name in the future.

Bud Garner. If I had to go to war on an Astroturf field, I always wanted Bud Garner and Pierre Alaire, for artificial infill turfs, on my side.

It's always fun to hear about guys who used to be on one of my crews winning awards in the minor leagues. In just the past few year, Tom Nielsen won an award in Class AAA Louisville, and Ryan Kaspitzki won an award in Class AA Dayton. Don LaBlanc of Nashua, New Hampshire, won the Atlantic League field of the 2003 season. You feel proud for these people.

You'll notice that only men are on my list. That's because groundskeeping historically has been a male-dominated profession. In giving speeches around the country, I often say the most important part of turf MANagement is the first three letters—the M-A-N. Now, I'm changing my speech to include W-O-M-A-N.

The Detroit Tigers hired Heather Nabozny as the first woman groundskeeper in the major leagues, and she is doing a fine job at Comerica Park. And for the first time ever, I had two women, Raechal Volkening and Abby McNeal, on our crew at the 2003 Super Bowl in San Diego. I'm sure we will see more and more women climb to the top of the profession as they work their way through the minor league and college ranks.

I often have felt that groundskeepers who do the best job tend to be loners. The mediocre ones form a club and cry on each other's shoulders, but the best ones do it themselves and take pride in a job well done. But as time goes by, I understand how valuable it is to have the support of your peers in the business.

I was blessed to have a great mentor in Emil Bossard, so I understand how important it is to pass the torch to the next generation. In 1981, I sat down at the old Muehlebach Hotel in downtown Kansas City with three great men—Harry Gill, groundskeeper for the Milwaukee Brewers; Dick Erickson, groundskeeper for the Minnesota Twins and Vikings; and Dr. Bill Daniels, an agronomist at Purdue University. Kent Kurtz, a professor at Cal-Poly, also helped us get organized.

At that meeting, we founded the Sports Turf Managers Association (STMA) to support and encourage professional groundskeepers on all levels. From that humble beginning, we now have more than 2,600 members. An annual award is presented in honor of each of the four founders. I am proud of mine, the George Toma Golden Rake Award. It's a way to honor hard work and then some, to distinguish the mediocre from the great.

However, some unresolved political issues hurt STMA in 2002. Sides were taken, and some of the best groundskeepers dropped out. That hurt me deeply. I asked everyone to pitch in and make it work, to let bygones be bygones. Our members must pull together to make it work for everyone. And I believe Steve Trusty, STMA director, has, and his staff will get it done.

Is there another Emil Bossard on the horizon? Not that I have seen. But with men like Don Follett, Eddie Mangan, Allen Sigwart, Mark Razum, Steve Wightman, Trevor Vance and Roger Bossard leading the way, I have great hope for the future of my profession.

CHAPTER 20

THE GEORGE P. TOMA HALL OF FAME

One of the greatest days of my life was August 3, 2001, when I was honored by the NFL Hall of Fame.

Even as a Hall of Fame honoree, however, I still have to take out the trash and mow the lawn. But I would like to take advantage of this accolade to create a Hall of Fame of my own. Of course, it goes without saying that guys such as Hank Stram and George Brett belong there and always will be in my hall. But this is my hall, so I also would like to include the unsung people who have meant so much to me.

My family. There would be no George Toma without my wife, Donna, keeping things under control back home. I am thankful that she is an avid sports fan and joins me on the road whenever possible.

As a matter of fact, we even planned our wedding around my work. We were married on February 6, 1981, near the Pro Bowl in Honolulu. As Donna says, at least we always know where we will be on our anniversary.

Chip, my oldest son, has been a successful groundskeeper in his own right and lives in Grain Valley, Missouri. He has three daughters, Brandy, Amanda and Alysse. My middle son, Rick, is vice president of the ERA Division of Cendant in New Jersey and has two daughters, Katie and Elizabeth. And Ryan, my youngest son, is a pilot and a student at Kansas State University.

Jim Steeg, NFL. I consider Jim the third-most important man in my life after my father and uncle. He is a man who always has time to talk things over with you and whom you can look up to for his devotion to the Super

One of the best parts of my Hall of Fame award ceremony was sharing it with my wife, Donna.

Bowl, Pro Bowl and everything else he has going. Jim is like a well-oiled machine. No one can shine his shoes. He is one of the best, and then some.

Billy Granholm, NFL. The late Billy Granholm preceded Jim Steeg with the NFL. I was fortunate enough to work with him on more than 30 Super Bowls. He previously had been an NFL equipment manager and seemed to know everyone in the league. He also did a lot for our servicemen overseas. Billy was a true gentleman who is greatly missed. What a tremendous boss.

Uncle John "King Kong" Noosh. Uncle John was a great role model for a young boy without a father, and he helped me get my start as a groundskeeper.

Jay Hinrich, stadium operations manager, Kansas City Royals. If I owned a business, I would have Jay run it for me. He is one of the top men I have worked for. He even picked me to be the godfather of his son, J.T. I just about cried when the Royals let him go, but he is doing a fine job at the University of Kansas.

Herk Robinson, Royals general manager. After reading about my many battles with Herk, some people may be surprised to find his name in my Hall of Fame. Herk makes the cut, not for his work with the Royals, but for being the best grass, tree and flower man in the Kansas City area. Herk and I have had our ups and downs, our ins and outs, but we still love each other.

Chuck Rubin, agent. I got tired of haggling over my salary with Herk Robinson, so I hired Chuck, who also is the agent for golfer Tom Watson. Chuck has always looked out for my best interests, although I still was the lowest-paid groundskeeper in the league when I left the Royals.

Show Ikeda, Japan. One of the most dedicated men I have ever met in athletic playing fields. His work ethic, desire and initiative cannot be beaten. He does a terrific job at the Super Bowl, Pro Bowl and American Bowl games in Japan.

John Wathan, player and manager, Royals. John was a true gentleman as a player and manager for the team. I am proud that he is the godfather of my son, Ryan.

In the spring of 2003, the Cleveland Indians were visiting the Minnesota Twins at Hammond Stadium in Fort Myers. I was pleasantly surprised to see a big, strapping young player come up to say hello—John's son, Dusty Wathan, whom I have known since he was a baby. One of the pleasures of being around baseball so long is seeing second- and third-generation players grow up to be good ballplayers themselves.

Al Zych, equipment manager, Royals. Al is one of the greatest people I have met in baseball. During spring training in Fort Myers, he used to have a row of lockers he called "Death Row." He put players in these lockers whom he knew would be the first to be sent down to the minors. Only one player ever made it from Death Row to the major leagues.

Walter Komatsubara, amateur groundskeeper (but a professional in my book). Walter is a retired Honolulu fire captain and Pacific Rim scout for the Boston Red Sox. He always goes the extra mile to help the young ballplayers of Hawaii.

Walter built the best pitching mound I have ever seen for a high school game in Hawaii, then taught the players how to maintain it. After the game, I looked it over, and there was not one thing wrong with it. It was the best mound I have seen in my 61 years in the game. Walter used to make clay mud balls for repairing the mound and home plate area, put them in covered five-gallon cans and give them to the high school kids to use.

Another time, he promised to build a new pitching mound in Maui for the state tournament. He finished that mound as promised, even though his mother passed away during that time. He paid attention to the details.

I have known Walter for 24 years, and you can't find a better person.

Nancy Gaba, secretary. Nancy was secretary for Charles Truitt of the Kansas City Royals from 1970 to 1972. We had just painted the field at Municipal Stadium for football when a few people from the Royals started walking across it. I told them, "Hit the road—the field is now the Chiefs'." A man we called Sky King, Ewing Kauffman's private pilot, went to Mr. Truitt's office and asked him to fire me. Nancy spoke up and said, "Who the hell are you?" Thanks, Nancy.

Bill Beck. Bill was an outstanding traveling secretary for the Royals, who moved on to the San Diego Padres and now the Florida Marlins. Bill is the best—he never lost the common touch.

Cedric Tallis, Kansas City Royals. Cedric, the first general manager, built the Royals from the ground up, making them one of the most successful expansion teams ever. He took care of everything from working with stadium architects to signing players. How can he not be in the Royals Hall of Fame? If you include people who put icing on the cake, include the guy who baked the cake.

Sara Croke, meteorologist. Sara and her company, Weather or Not, kept me on top of the latest conditions. One time, her radar broke down, so Sara got in her car, followed the storm and relayed the information to our crew at Kauffman Stadium. Thanks, Sara.

Bob Sprenger, public relations, Kansas City Chiefs. What a great person. He never lost the common touch.

Bob Woolford, vice president, Shawnee Mission Medical Center. Bob came up with the slogan "and then some," which to me separates the great from the mediocre. Bob is a great man, and I owe him a lot. Thanks, Bob.

Jim Carnes, owner, International Seed. We used to call him Uncle Jim, because he became like a father to me and my crew. Jim never showed up at the stadium without bringing along food for the kids. He was one man you could always talk to and he has done so much for me and my family.

Lee County (Florida) grounds crew. I have been working spring training since 1948 and have never had a better experience than with the Lee County Sports Complex grounds crew and the Minnesota Twins. Everything is done first class, thanks to Bill Hammond, John Yarborough and Terry Ryan, general manager of the Twins.

Rush Limbaugh, special events, Royals. Yes, that Rush Limbaugh. What a great man. Old Rush and I got along good, because we were the low men on the totem pole. George Brett loved Rush, and Rush didn't have much money in those days, so George would give him things. Al Zych used to take care of Rush and me with sandwiches and spaghetti red dishes. Rush has never forgotten those days, and neither have I.

My complete Hall of Fame would fill several books, but I'll leave you with several more names who deserve to be mentioned:

Santa Claus Joe. The recently deceased Joe Hess was a fixture in right field general admission at Kauffman Stadium and the No. 1 fan of the Royals. He was a legend in Kansas City, as well as a terrific gentleman.

Chuck Brasher. Thanks for sharing both your vast knowledge of trees and those tasty crappie filets from Stockton Dam.

Smokey Olsen. Smokey was my longtime assistant with both the A's and Royals.

Marvin and Patsy Gretencord. This farmer and schoolteacher from Johnson County, Kansas, baked wonderful cookies and carrot cake for our grounds crew.

Cleveland Indians' groundskeeping legend Emil Bossard.

NFL coaches. I have been fortunate to be around some of the all-time greats. The ones who will always stand out to me are Hank Stram, Paul Wiggin, Marv Levy, Frank Ganz, Marty Schottenheimer, Weeb Ewbank, Bill Parcells, Chuck Noll, John Madden, June Jones, Mike Ditka, Walt Michaels, Tom Flores, and Bill Walsh.

NFL players. Most of these guys ended up in either the Chiefs or the NFL Hall of Fame, as well as mine: Ed Budde, Jim Tyrer, Buck Buchanan, Bobby Bell, WIllie Lanier, Howie Long, Jan Stenerud, Nick Lowery, Jack Rudnay, Len Dawson, Emmitt Smith, Brett Favre, Marcus Allen, Ronnie Lott, and Mike Garrett.

Kansas City A's—Owner Charlie O. Finley, George Selkirk, Jack Fette, and crew members Henry Wheat, the Chouteau family, the Armstrong family, the Bruce family, Melvin Duncan, and all grounds crew members.

Kansas City Royals and Chiefs—Owners Ewing Kauffman and Lamar Hunt, and from my crews, Scott Martin, Andre Bruce, Doug Schallenberg of the Chiefs, the Dahany twins, the Vaughn twins, Melvin Duncan, Johnny Williams, John Martin, Smokey Olsen, Wilford Bruce, Roland Bruche, Terry Porch, Chiefs equipment managers: Bobby Yarborough, John Phillips, Mike Davidson; Royals equipment managers: Chuck Hawke, Mike Burkhalter, Tommy Walsh, John Schmiedler; Chiefs trainers: Wayne Rudy, Dane Kendall; Royals trainers: Mickey Cobb, Paul McGannon, Steve Morrow; Royals

An outstanding crew helped me turn Municipal Stadium into a showplace. Kneeling (from left) are Kenny Chouteau, me, and Jim Chouteau. Standing (from left) are Charlie McComber, Henry Wheat, Tom Weakley, Frank Merideth, Donald Chouteau, Ray Haywood, and Larry Chouteau.

Scouts: Art Stewart, Jay Hankins; Royals front office: Dale Rohr, Joe Grigoli, Wanda Clark, Betty Bax, and Chris Rice.

Jimmy Warfield of the Cleveland Indians, now deceased—A great one—who never lost the common touch of a player—ground crew favorite.

Personal—Dr. Jim Mertz, Dr. Darrell Davis, Dr. Austenfeld, Dr. Rolfe Becker and Dr. Andrew Jacobs.

Crew members—I have been in this business for 60-some years, and I never took an application. I could tell by just looking at you if you were a good worker. I didn't have to know your background. I have never fired anybody, and I never had anybody work for me. They all worked with me.

There you have it. You may never see these names in Cooperstown or Canton, but they always will be at the top of my list.

CHAPTER 21

GRASS GROWING 101

By now, you have read my opinions on everything from female groundskeepers to artificial turf to baseball owners. I'm sure you must be wondering, "When is he going to tell me how to grow better grass in my own lawn?"

I get asked that question all the time, and it's the one I hate to answer. The problem is, what I do goes against just about every piece of advice you would get from the experts in the field. I refuse to go by the book.

Take the field at old Municipal Stadium. In the early 1960s, I used to seed in August, fertilize around Labor Day and then fertilize again around Thanksgiving. I thought, "Gee, here I am sitting here eating turkey. That grass has helped me all year, so it should have a good Thanksgiving, too." So I went out and fertilized.

A lot of Midwest agronomists used to make fun of me, saying, "What's that guy doing now?" But today, most of them will tell you to fertilize around Labor Day and again in November. All I know is, it worked for me.

Now, Herk Robinson of the Royals is the master of going by the book. Herk has studied every book on the market, and you won't find a better lawn than the one at his home. Watching Herk work with his hands in the soil is like watching Ted Williams swing the bat. He's amazing.

But that's just not my style. I am aware of two groundskeepers who have been successful going against the book, Eddie Mangan and me. What the book says, we throw away.

So I will leave the grass growing instructions to the agronomists. Instead I'll share some of the ideas—orthodox and unorthodox—that have worked for me over the years.

One thing I have done for years is to "pregerminate" seed to give it a head start before planting. This can make all of the difference in the world in an emergency or when trying to quickly convert between sports.

I learned my "recipe" for pregerminating grass seed by trial and error, not a horticultural textbook. Here it is, with the help of Dr. James R. Watson:

> For pregerminating a vast amount of seed, use 55 gallon barrels. At the top of the barrel put a spigot. Now the top of the barrel becomes the bottom of the barrel. The bottom of the barrel is cut out. Cut flyscreen to fit tight on the bottom of the barrel, also placing some heavy hardware cloth on wire mesh. Place the barrel on top of a concrete block, four by four. One barrel will hold 150 pounds of rye grass. Mix a solution of PBI Gordon's Launch in a pail. Start to fill the barrel with water, adding the Launch solution. Fill the barrel up to six inches from the top. The wet seed will swell. Mix seed, or if you have an air compressor with a long pipe, blow air to mix the seed. Do this at 8:00 a.m. and again at the end of the day, then drain the barrel and fill with water.
>
> On day two, in the morning, drain the barrel and then fill it again. Before you leave for the day, drain the barrel but do not fill it. On day three, fill the barrel with water in the morning, and before you leave, empty the barrel. If this is done in a warm place, it will enhance the germination. Keep a close look on the seed to see if it is starting to grow a white fuzz. This usually happens on the fourth day. Dump the seed on the concrete floor, and rake it out. It

might be ready then. When it is ready, mix the seed with Milorganite fertilizer. Use one shovel of seed to two shovels of Milorganite, or use calcined clay. Trial mix this so the seed will flow easily out of a spreader. For large amounts, use a cement mixer. You can also punch a few small holes in the bag, place it in a garbage can and follow the same above procedure. For a small amount, one can place this seed in a nylon paint screen net, or even panty hose and put it in a pail and follow the same procedure as above.

Usually rye grass and Bermuda will germinate in three to four days this way. We have seeded on Sundays and cut the grass on Friday, painted on Saturday, and played on Sunday. In San Diego, at Super Bowl XXIII, we seeded on Thursday and the grass was two inches high on Monday. With blue grass, one will have to follow the above procedure for seven to ten days.

I have never been more proud of any turf than the two practice fields my son Chip and I built for the Chiefs at their training camp at William Jewell College in Liberty, Missouri. The college already had beautiful grass, but when it rained, the fields flooded because of the clay base. Jack Steadman, president of the Chiefs, gave us a budget of $44,000 to rebuild both fields.

The first thing we did was send a sample of the soil to Texas A&M University for testing. They said it was the same texture as the clay soil used on pitching mounds and around home plate areas. To make it work, they said, we would need a mixture of 13 inches of sand to one inch of soil. But our budget would allow us to buy only five inches of sand.

I call our solution the "Chip Toma/Dr. James Watson Milkshake System." We rototilled the fields and applied gypsum as deep as it would go. Next, we installed drainage pipes about every 20 feet lengthwise, back-filled the trenches with pea gravel and humped the sand. Then we added three inches of sand and rototilled it five inches deep, ending up with three inches of sand and two inches of soil, which we blended in. Next, we put the other two inches of sand on top and harrowed it in. Finally, we sprigged in the grass, and within six weeks, the field was ready for training camp.

There was one small problem. We had gone $3,000 over budget on each field, and Steadman called me in his office and chewed me out. But I had the last laugh. Right before the first practice, there was a cloud burst, with about four and three quarters inches of rain. Coach John Mackovic had more than a hundred players in camp, and they never missed a practice all through two-a-days.

After the Chiefs broke camp, William Jewell and Liberty High School played football and soccer on those fields, the state football championships were played there—and they had grass all the way through. The great irony is that our $25,000 fields played great in the rain, while our two $100,000 water removal machines sat idle at Arrowhead Stadium.

My point is this: The people who install and maintain a field are far more important than the money you pour into it. It's heartbreaking to me to see how bad the field was at the Meadowlands. How in the world can you spend $120,000 to sod a field, have it fall apart and sod it again in the same week? This is the biggest disaster for natural grass. Who suffers? The players, the owners and the taxpayers. I am not picking on the Meadowlands, but it hurts me to see natural grass suffer and it hurts me to hear

TV announcers calling the Denver Broncos' new field (in November 2003 for a soccer game) as bare as a bowling alley. Again, did we get too sophisticated with our playing fields? Is a $25,000 playing field better than the multi-million dollar fields or are they the cheapest advertisement for artificial turf? We need to go back to the basics.

Compare the Meadowlands to Holman Stadium in Nashua, New Hampshire. There was no drainage and a two-man crew. Yet even after playing Atlantic League baseball, American Legion and Babe Ruth baseball, and college and high school football on the field, it still looks great for the annual Thanksgiving Day game. But in the NFL and major colleges, they have eight to 10 people working on a field, and it will still fall apart. We're experimenting too much with the taxpayers' money.

Now that we lay sod instead of growing grass from seed, a lot of the fault lies with the sod growers. When the Houston Astros moved to their new ballpark, it had to be sodded twice in the same week. When the Super Bowl was played at Sun Devil Stadium in Tempe, Arizona, we had to send back 13 truckloads of sod because it was cut wrong. Sod growers must do a better job. The Meadowlands and Sun Devil Stadium both were sodded twice in one week in 2002.

It all starts with the base, and a lot of times, contractors cheat with the soil and sand mixture. That makes it difficult to do a good job of sodding. When we come in to lay sod, we need to know there is a good base without any problems.

Steve Wightman and his crew at Qualcomm Stadium in San Diego showed me some pictures of some sod they had laid—it looked worse than Grandma's quilt. The sod we used there for the 2003 Super Bowl was first rate, the best, but the seams fell apart during transportation. Sod farms need to do a better job of shipping and delivering their product.

I remember one time when I took delivery of some poor sod that looked bad on the field. Before the game, I told the crew to look at all of the buses in the parking lot and said, "These people must be coming to wash their clothes on the world's largest washing board," because that is what the field looked like.

A lot of people say, "George, you're complaining." I say, "Hey, this is professional sports. You have to give the player the best field to perform on and a field of beauty and do it without wasting the owner's money."

We have lost the art of growing grass somewhere along the way. Maybe we are getting lazy. I mean, come on. Let's get back to basics and grow grass again. Again, bad sod and a bad field are the cheapest advertising for artificial turf. How many times in the past few years have major fields had to be resodded twice in the same week? Come on—we have to get better. There is no resodding with artificial turf.

Part of the problem is the newfangled grasses they keep experimenting with. Several years ago, Sports Grass was all the rage. It is simply natural grass interwoven among artificial turf fibers with a backing. I had my doubts from the beginning. I saw it at the farm where they grow it and told my crew, "If you can find a fiber in the top inch of the turf, I'll give you $1,000." The fibers laid flat, and when a player ran, he took a chunk out of it.

Both the Green Bay Packers and Baltimore Ravens converted to Sports Grass and soon regretted their decisions. I told Bill Paprocki of Sports Grass, "I don't think it will work. You will top-dress this thing, and the blades will fall down and the grass will shear off." He called later to say the players hated it and they were taking it out. The

Packers also replaced it at Lambeau Field. Bill is one of my favorite people. He had been a great help to me, and he sure knows athletic fields.

Allen Sigwart tried Sports Grass at Joe Robbie Stadium in Miami, and it came up looking like toupees. Allen is one of the best groundskeepers in the game, and seeing his field like that was very disheartening. He replaced it with Eddie Woerner's 419 Bermuda grown on plastic. It looked great, and it was less expensive. Once again, we are getting too sophisticated for our own good.

Some of the best sod I have ever seen is what we put on the concrete floor of the New Orleans Superdome for a preseason game between the Saints and Packers in 1999. The rolls were seven feet wide and 41 feet long and weighed 4,000 pounds. Each piece was perfect, like someone had sliced it with a straight razor. We need more men like Woerner. You can't beat his sod grown on plastic.

The Saints and Packers both scrimmaged on that field and never dented it. On Saturday, the Southern University marching band rehearsed on it and didn't faze it. After the game, coach Mike Ditka said, "George, sweep the field, cut it and we'll play a doubleheader tonight." After the game ended, it took only eight hours to remove the turf and have the stadium floor ready for a convention.

I have followed three simple rules throughout my career, and they have served me well:

1. Give the players a safe surface on which to play. The cheapest insurance for an athlete from preschool to the pros is a safe playing field.

2. Make the field aesthetically pleasing for fans in the stands and watching on television.

3. Do the first two things without taking too much money out of the pockets of owners and taxpayers.

What variety of grass should you plant? It all depends on where you live and how much work you want to put into your lawn. The main factor is whether you live in an area where warm-season or cool-season varieties thrive—or in the transition zone, where growing either can be a challenge.

Kentucky bluegrass may be the most common variety, with a number of good blends of seed on the market. It can provide a great-looking lawn in the spring and fall but needs frequent watering during hot summers. It tends to spread out and fill in bare spots in the lawn. Creeping red fescue and chewing fescue do well in shady areas but do require some sun each day. Perennial ryegrass is another option to establish a lawn quickly, but it often dies in the summer. A lot of homeowners are experimenting with native grasses such as buffalo grass, which require little moisture.

The choices today, unlike when I started out in the business, are almost limitless. My best advice? Look for a lawn in your area that you particularly admire, find out what type of grass it is and ask your local lawn and garden retailer about how difficult it is to grow and maintain.

Here are a few tips you can use on your own lawn. The most important thing is to plant good grass seed—you will always get your money's worth. Go to a reliable nursery and get some George P. Toma Pennington brand grass seed, or pick up Pennington Tournament grass seed at Wal-Mart (just look for my picture on the label). That's the one I use at the Super Bowl.

In warm climates, try my favorite, Princess 77 Bermuda grass seed. Follow up with lawn care products from PBI Gordon, an employee-owned business in Kansas City. You will have the best lawn for the least amount of effort.

Remember, I usually find a way to go against the book. But you can't go wrong taking the advice of my friends at Pennington Seed, the best grass seed company in the business for my money:

Pennington's Tips for the Home Lawn

New Lawn Development

Pulverize the soil completely by spading or plowing. If soil tests have been conducted, apply fertilizer at the recommended rate. If soil tests have not been conducted, apply lime and a complete lawn fertilizer available at your lawn and garden dealer, apply lime and fertilizer at recommended rates and according to directions. Work lime and fertilizer evenly into the soil, then level the soil. Sow the grass seed; then rake, harrow, or otherwise work the seed into the soil no more than one-fourth inch. Keep the area well watered until the seeds have germinated and the seedlings have grown sufficiently to establish a lawn, then water as needed.

Overseeding or Reseeding

Fertilize as recommended in the first step, although it is not necessary to work the fertilizer into the soil. Mow or clip the existing grass as closely as possible. Rake, harrow lightly, aerate or otherwise scarify the soil where the existing grass is growing to allow the seed to make contact with the soil. The existing grass will not be adversely affected.

Undesirable Lawn

When you have a lawn with undesirable grasses, you may use the following method or ridding your lawn of these grasses and establishing a desirable lawn.

1. During any growing season, spray the established undesirable lawn with a non-selective herbicide, labeled for lawn use, following the directions on the label.

2. After lawn turns brown, follow instructions in step one or step two above.

Improving Bare Spots

First mow closely, then remove leaves, dead grass and other debris. Rake bare spots to prepare the seed bed. Then follow fertilizer and planting instructions as outlined above.

Tip of the Day

Whether you are using lawn seed, fertilizers, chemicals, or any other product, a good rule of thumb is to always read the product label for the product name, active ingredients, usage directions, and caution instructions. You will be surprised how many questions you can answer by reading a product's label.

Another question I get asked all the time is how baseball groundskeepers create the beautiful patterns in the outfield and infield grass. The secret is a heavy roller attached to the back of the mower. One simple pattern is to first mow in a straight line away from the infield to create a light stripe, then back in a straight line toward the infield for a darker strip.

These can get fancier by making crisscross patterns at right angles to each other, creating contrasting patterns in the infield and outfield, or other intricate patterns. The best groundskeepers vary the patterns between home stands or even between games. Mowing grass may be seem like a basic chore, but it's one more way in which good groundskeepers show their creativity and make the game fun for fans in the stands and watching at home on television. For patterns, Dave Mellor of the Boston Red Sox is the best.

Most sports fans judge groundskeepers by how well they grow grass, which is fair enough. But those of us in the business know that maintaining dirt is far more challenging. In baseball, only three men play on grass. Six defenders—as well as the batter—are on dirt. Roger Bossard of the White Sox grew up in the business, learning it from his father, Gene, and grandfather, Emil. But Roger said his dad never let him water the dirt at Comiskey Park until he was well into his teens. When it comes to dirt infields, Roger leads the pack.

We always had excellent infields in Kansas City, a mixture of 40 percent sand, 30 percent silt and 30 percent clay. Infield dirt from the Jim Kelsey Dirt Farm in New Jersey is the best I have seen in 61 years in the game. Once again, the man who works the dirt often is far more important than the dirt itself.

I guess that's why they call me the Nitty Gritty Dirt Man.

CHAPTER 22

GROUNDSKEEPING BY DECEIT

Bill Veeck used to say a good groundskeeper was the 10th man on the field and was worth five to seven victories a season.

I used to kid Gene Bossard when he worked for Veeck at Comiskey Park in Chicago. Gene was the master of such pranks as freezing baseballs before games to slow them down. I'm convinced Gene won 20 games a year for the White Sox, but he never got that million-dollar contract. I'm not saying any of us ever broke the rules of the game, but we were not above bending them here and there to give our home team an edge.

My old friend Joe Mooney of the Boston Red Sox was legendary. He started out as bat boy for the Scranton (Pennsylvania) Miners, and to the best of my knowledge, he was the only bat boy ever to get thrown out of a ballpark. That's because he had an incredible knack for picking up the catcher's signs and relaying them to the batter.

The Kansas City A's needed every edge they could get. Back in the 1960s, Alvin Dark managed the team and Bobby Hoffman was a coach. Out in left field was a tall tower with a Butternut Bread sign and a digital clock. It also was a perfect signal tower.

When the game started, Bobby would climb up into the right centerfield scoreboard and steal the catcher's sign. If it was a fastball, the clock may read "8:00," with two dots. But if he called for a breaking ball, it would read "8.00," with one dot missing or the lights in the pen of Charlie O., the mascot mule. If the lantern was on in the pen, it was a breaking pitch. If the lantern was off, it was a fastball.

One day Hank Bauer, who was managing the Baltimore Orioles, said, "George, something is fishy. They're getting my signs." I said, "They may be getting them, but you're still winning." Even if you know what pitch is coming, you still have to hit the ball.

We had a few other somewhat legal tricks at Municipal Stadium. When a good bunter came to town, we graded the baselines so the bunts would roll foul. We made the batter's box hard so Ted Williams couldn't get a foothold and center field as hard as asphalt for Mickey Mantle. When the White Sox came in, with speedsters such as Nellie Foxx and Luis Aparicio, we made it soft around first base so they couldn't get a good jump to steal second.

But with Charlie Finley's pennant porch and wacky ideas, nothing we did could ever top our owner's shenanigans. Even with our help, the A's never won consistently until Charlie moved them to Oakland.

The fun continued at Kauffman Stadium with the Royals. We had players like George Brett, Amos Otis and Hal McRae, and the great Charlie Lau as our batting coach. We moved the batter's box back four or six inches for Hal and Amos so they could get a better look at the ball. The batters, of course, would wipe out the line with their cleats and gain a few more inches.

A traded player can be a groundskeeper's worst enemy. When catcher Buck Martinez got traded to Milwaukee, he tipped off manager George Bamberger on what we were doing. I remember umpire Bill Kunkel pulling out a tape measure and checking it when the Brewers came to town.

Kauffman Stadium in Kansas City remains one of the most beautiful parks in all of baseball.

I'll tell you this: Anything we ever did in Kansas City pales in comparison with the legendary Bossard family at old Comiskey Park in Chicago. Where do you start? Back in 1967, when my old friend Eddie Stanky was managing the White Sox, he demanded that the grass in front of the short stop be left long, because his shortstop had limited range. But he had a good second baseman, so he wanted that area cut short.

The Bossards cut the outfield grass long to slow down the ball when they had poor fielders and cut it short when they had speedy hitters with the "Go-Go Sox." They even put extra paint on the foul lines to help their good bunters keep the ball fair.

The area in front of home plate was dug up and soaked with water when knuckleballers such as Hoyt Wilhelm were on the mound for the White Sox. But if the other team threw a knuckleball pitcher, the dirt was dug up, mixed with gasoline and burned to make it hard as concrete. The pitching mounds in the visitors' bullpen were raised or lowered from the standard 10 inches to throw the relievers off their rhythms.

When the last Bossard retires from groundskeeping—which I hope never happens—their family could write quite a book.

It's much harder to give your team an edge in football, although Hank Stram once asked me to try. One time the Chiefs were going to play San Diego, and Hank said to me, "You know, San Diego has Lance Alworth. We have to wet down the sidelines about 15 feet in so that when Alworth runs down the sideline and has to make that cut, he falls on his fanny."

We did wet it down, but when Alworth made his cut, he didn't fall down. Our cornerback Freddie "The Hammer" Williamson fell down, and Alworth went all the way. The next game, I asked Hank how he wanted the field, and he said, "Oh George, keep it hard, keep it hard, keep it hard."

I often have said that job one for any groundskeeper is to provide a safe place for athletes to play. But if you can do that while giving your team a bit of an edge, it makes the games all that much more fun.

CHAPTER 23

AND THEN SOME

After my father died when I was 10, my mother went to work in the local bakery. I can only imagine what it was like for her to slave in front of a hot oven all day while raising a family and dealing with the loss of her husband. But not once did she ever complain.

My family always taught me to give my employer 100 percent and more. That has been my philosophy from when I worked on farms in my teens to working on championship fields in my 70s.

As much as I lived this philosophy of life, I never was able to adequately express it to other people. Then, in 1991, I received a letter from Bob Woolford, vice president of Shawnee Mission Medical Center in suburban Kansas City. He said he was at a Royals game and admired my crew, because we did our job "and then some."

Those three words clicked with me, and I have been using them ever since. In fact, the STMA award named after me officially is called the "George Toma And Then Some Golden Rake Award," thanks to Bob Woolford.

Nothing makes me prouder than to see other people adopt this motto and find success in their own lives. One of those people is my great friend Rush Limbaugh. I am proud that he included me in writing about the five secrets of success. I include his comments here not to brag on what I have done but to show how he has used the same approach to become the most-listened-to radio host in the nation. I don't think anyone has done a better job of summing up what is meant by, "and then some." Here is Rush:

"A few years ago, I went to the Super Bowl in Atlanta, between the Buffalo Bills and Dallas Cowboys, as the invited guest of Steve Sabol of NFL Films. At their pre-production meeting, I listened to Sabol fire up the cameramen, the crew that would be stationed all over the Georgia Dome. He quoted something that his dad, Ed Sabol, had always told their staff and was obviously the standard at NFL Films: 'Finish like a pro.' In other words, don't forget to go flat-out—no matter if the game's 25-zip with 30 seconds to play. There still may be a great play out there. Give up on nothing. Finish like a pro.

"I pondered that as we went out on the field. There I spotted the man I knew as the chief groundskeeper for the Royals and Chiefs in the late '70s and early '80s when I worked in Kansas City. It was George Toma, now the official groundskeeper for the National Football League at Super Bowls and Pro Bowls... And he was on his hands and knees, crawling on the sidelines. Photographers and the halftime entertainment were waiting to go out and rehearse the pregame show, and he was kneeling among them.

"'George, what are you doing?' I asked. He answered: 'I'm getting the field ready for the game.' He had tape all over his knuckles. He was on his knees, using tape to pick up lint. I said, 'This is the sidelines!' He shot back: 'Biggest game in the world, Rush. You've got TV cameras from all over the world here.' I said, 'But George, the minute you finish, the band will be walking all over here.'

"And I'll never forget his reply: 'You do everything you can and then just a little more.'

"I thought I'd seen a vision. Here were two people at the top of their game, Steve Sabol and George Toma, the absolute best at what they do. And both of them were doing things most people would consider a total waste of time. Most people would have been satisfied with far less, but they were not. Their standards were higher. Their personal best required them to do more.

I consider Jim Steeg of the NFL the third most important man in my life, after only my father and my uncle.

"It's not just talent that produces success. It's demanding more of yourself than anyone else does. This approach can start with you right now, today, wherever you are—while you're in school, looking for a job, on any job, preparing for any challenge. Get there earlier, stay later, produce it better. Study harder, practice longer, go beyond what's 'required.' When you make this your habit and your mindset, you have to put yourself on the road to success. A route, I may add, that is always self-directed."

I was doing some work at old Foxboro Stadium, and coach Dick McPherson asked me to speak to his players the night before their big game against the New York Jets. I discussed how the field would play, then told the players, "Do your job, and then some. That is what distinguishes the mediocre from the great."

The next day, the Patriots were driving for the winning score, but the Jets held them at the goal line. Some of the players came up to me the next day and said, "How are you doing, and then some?"

I said jokingly, "You know what? Bruce Coslet, the coach of the Jets, called me after I spoke to you, and I gave the Jets the same speech. They listened, and they stopped you on four downs."

I could never begin to repay all of the people who showed that "and then some" attitude to me. I would like to thank God, my parents, George and Mary Toma; my sister, Catherine; my uncle and aunt, John and Eva Yarrish; and my coach in the NFL and in life, Jim Steeg. I owe you everything.

It's been a great life, from the coal mines to being honored at the Hall of Fame. I plan to keep on working as long as the good Lord allows. The next time you tune in the Super Bowl, remember that George Toma gave it everything he had—and then some.

APPENDIX A

Resumé

GEORGE P. TOMA

Born: February 2, 1929, Edwardsville, Pennsylvania

Married: Wife Donna

Children: Chip (December 17, 1956)   Construction

Rick (November 12, 1964)   Vice President, ERA Division of Cendant

Ryan (June 12, 1983)   Pilot and Student/ Kansas State University

1942	Started work at Artillery Park for Wilkes-Barre Barons, Class A Eastern League
1946	Named head groundskeeper for Wilkes-Barre Indians, Class A Eastern League
1948-50	Worked with Emil Bossard, world-renowned groundskeeper for Cleveland Indians, in Driver, Virginia, Marietta, Florida, and Daytona Beach, Florida
1951-53	Military service in Korean War; discharged as sergeant first class
1954	Head groundskeeper, Wilkes-Barre Barons, Class A Eastern League
1957	Nov. 1, named head groundskeeper for Kansas City Athletics, American League, Municipal Stadium
1963	Head groundskeeper, Kansas City Chiefs, National Football League; contract remains with Athletics

1966	Chosen by NFL to prepare field for first Super Bowl and has been in charge of fields for every Super Bowl and Pro Bowl. NFL natural and artificial turf consultant, prepared fields for playoff game with problems, consulted with NFL teams
1969-95	Named head groundskeeper, Kansas City Royals, American League, Royals/Kauffman Stadium; maintained position with Chiefs and added director of landscaping at Harry S. Truman Sports Complex
1973	Appeared in major film *Black Sunday*, starring Robert Shaw
1982	Featured in *Sports Illustrated* article, "Nitty Gritty Dirt Man"
1984	Named consultant for Los Angeles Olympics at the Rose Bowl, Los Angeles Coliseum and Los Angeles Junior College for track events, soccer and field hockey
1985	Began working NFL overseas American Bowl games in London, Tokyo, Berlin, Barcelona, Mexico City and Monterrey, Mexico
1992	Named to John Madden's "All-Madden Team"
1994	Assisted Dr. James R. Watson at all nine venues for World Cup Soccer, running the venues at Soldier Field in Chicago and Silverdome in Pontiac, Michigan
1995	Received "Advanced Science Award" from International Hall of Fame of Science for advanced seed germination process

1996	Re-laid turf field at Olympic Stadium for Atlanta Olympics; laid 13,500 yards of sod in 24 hours, with 12 hours of sod bed preparation
1996	Named to Kansas City's "Walk of Stars" for local sports figures
1997	Spent three weeks in Gezer, Israel, building the only regulation baseball field in Israel for the 1997 Maccabee Games, worldwide Jewish Olympics
1999	Rehabilitated baseball field for Nashua Pride baseball team in Nashua, New Hampshire; featured in segments of *Goin' Deep* sports magazine show on Fox Sports
2000	Consulted for Ladd Stadium resodding for Senior Bowl game; artificial turf consultant for NCAA football championship in New Orleans Superdome; consulted on building and maintenance program for football and soccer practice fields for the University of Hawaii, Manoa campus
2001	Filmed ESPN promotional spot for *SportsCenter* television show; consulted with Newark Bears baseball team in Newark, New Jersey; consulted for Lee County baseball field in Fort Myers, Florida; participated in ACE Hardware Picture Perfect Lawn contest; received Dan Reeves Pioneer Award at Pro Football Hall of Fame in Canton, Ohio; renovated War Memorial Stadium field in Maui for University of Hawaii
2002	Featured on television program *Hometown Heroes* on Time-Warner Cable in Kansas

	City; worked spring training for Minnesota Twins in Fort Myers, Florida; received award from Greater Kansas City Sports Commission; worked on War Memorial Stadium in Maui, Hawaii
2003	Oversaw conversion of Aloha Stadium in Honolulu to FieldTurf; expert witness in turf grass cases; speaker at numerous colleges about turfgrass management; consultant for many Major League Baseball and NFL teams; received numerous awards from Sports Turf Managers Association (STMA); Honorary lifetime member of STMA; Man of the Year awards from cities and states; namesake of George Toma Gold Rake Award to STMA member for dedication, hard work and the "And Then Some" attitude

Appendix B

Hall of Fame Acceptance Speech

August 3, 2001

Thank you. Honored guests, ladies and gentlemen:

What a surprise, some 60 years ago from marking football fields in the anthracite coal region of Edwardsville, Pennsylvania, with screened white coal ashes and black coal dust on snow-covered fields. Here I am today, unbelievable. It would not have happened without the help of my family, Mr. Lamar Hunt and Jack Steadman. A sincere special thanks to Commissioner Pete Rozelle, Tex Schramm, the Hall of Fame committee and all the people who have worked with me.

Every blade of grass has an angel bending over it, whispering, "Grow, grow." I'm like a blade of grass, with so many saints helping me along the way. A very sincere special thanks to Commissioner Paul Tagliabue, my six All-Pro quarterbacks whom I was a recipient of their touchdown passes of help—Bill Granholm, Val Pinchbeck, Don Weiss, Roger Goodell, Joe Brown and agronomist Dr. James R. Watson; and in today's materialistic world, a man who has not lost the common touch, my coach and NFL father, Jim Steeg. Yes, Jim, the NFL shield will be with me always and over my heart.

To the NFL and football Hall of Fame—may all of you be repaid a thousandfold for your kindness. And to all of you, may all your good fortunes be as numerous as blades of grass; seed, the gift of life.

Appendix C

Kansas City Sports Commission Speech

Thank you, honored guests, ladies and gentlemen, plus the Kansas City Sports Commission. What a surprise! Some 60 years ago from marking and caring for baseball and football fields in the anthracite coal region of Edwardsville, Pennsylvania, with white coal ashes and black coal dust on snow-covered fields. Here I am today in front of all the great people of the Kansas City area.

It would not have happened without the help of my family. A sincere special thank to the Kansas City Sports Commission. Working from 1942 to 1954 for the Wilkes-Barre Indians of the Class A Eastern Leagues; on to the 1955 Buffalo Bisons of the AAA International League for Detroit; 1956 to 1957, Charleston, West Virginia of the AAA American Association. Then the biggest day of my life arrived, November 1, 1957, when I was named head groundskeeper for the Kansas City Athletics—the greatest sports city on earth! I love Kansas City. How lucky can one be?

As I always said, there would be no George P. Toma without the people I have worked for and with. Please bear with me, there are so many special people who have helped: The Kansas City A's' George Selkirk, who scouted me; along with Bob Wachter; Park Carroll; Arnold Johnson; Jack Fette; Toro's tex/champion and agronomist, Dr. James R. Watson; Charles O. Finley of the A's.

Kansas City Spurs soccer's John Latshaw and John Tyler; Kansas City Chiefs' Lamar Hunt, Jack Steadman, Jim Schaaf, Bobby Yarborough, Wayne Rudy and Hank Stram; the Royals' Mr. and Mrs. Kauffman, Cedric Tallis,

Charles Truitt, Phil Koury, Mickey Cobb, George Brett and Al Zych, who fed Rush Limbaugh and me; and my sons, Chip, Rick and Ryan, who all have worked at the stadium.

A special thanks to all of the grounds crews I have worked with. The only thing I believe I missed out on is not having the opportunity to work for one of the great businessmen of our nation, baseball owner and baseball's biggest fan, David Glass, another Ewing Kauffman.

It wasn't always easy to work in Kansas City. Before I took the job, I checked with my mentor, the greatest groundskeeper who ever lived, Emil Bossard of Cleveland. I told him I had an interview with Kansas City and he said, "Stay away from there! The spring would flood us out, the summer would bake us out. DON'T GO THERE!"

I had other opportunities, too—Denver, Yankee Stadium—but there is only one place like Kansas City. As I look back, this would not have happened without the help of the great people around the neighborhood of 22nd and Brooklyn—their wonderful children who became the crew, the Bruce family, the Armstrongs, the Duncans, the Conways, the Chouteau family.

We can't forget the Kansas City Monarchs, with Buck O'Neil; the Ban Johnson League with Mr. Don Motley and Les Milgram; the only chief, mayor Roe Bartle, who personally made sure on a flight to Atlanta that I did not take the Atlanta Braves and Falcons job. The mayor used both seats next to me on that flight.

A special thanks to commissioner Pete Rozelle of the National Football League and the current commissioner, Paul Tagliabue and Jim Steeg. And yes, a lot of this wouldn't have happened without the help of the best and the fairest, the outstanding Kansas City-area sportscasters, writers and fans.

To the Kansas City Sports Commission, everyone here and also the best people of the world, your fingerprints are all over this award, and may all of you be repaid a thousandfold for your kindness to me and my family. To all of you, may all your good fortunes be as numerous as blades of grass. Kansas City area, the gift of sports with great fans and owners and players, God bless you all.

APPENDIX D

STMA Open Letter

Dear STMA Member,

I am constantly amazed at how far our association—and our profession—have come.

When I started out in the 1940s, it was every man for himself. Fortunately, two great men, Emil Bossard of the Cleveland Indians and Dr. James R. Watson of Toro—took me under their wings. Without them, there would be no George Toma. I also leaned heavily on Joe Mooney in Boston, Dick Erickson in Minnesota and Pat Sandarone in Baltimore.

Other groundskeepers of my generation were not so fortunate. That's why Dick, Harry Gill of Milwaukee and Dr. Bill Daniels of Purdue University sat down at the Hotel Muehlebach in downtown Kansas City one day and founded the Sports Turf Managers Association. From those humble beginnings, we have grown to more than 26,000 members.

Without rehashing all of the details, our association hit a bump in the road in 2002. Things were said, sides were taken and many of our best groundskeepers dropped out of STMA. That has hurt me deeply, and I guarantee it is something Harry Gill would never have wanted to see happen.

Let me say this as simply as I can: It's time to let bygones be bygones and help rebuild a stronger, better STMA. Because the bottom line is, the STMA is your organization. The only reason it exists to help each of us improve our skills and the reputation of our proud profession. But we must pull together, from Steve Trusty and the board on down to the newest members. Whether they are certified or not, we must give it the "and then some."

Remember, we have all kinds of members, from those with advanced college degrees to those who didn't graduate from high school. Our association is big enough to accommodate everyone. And the members who are doing a great job at the high school, college, minor league or parks and recreation levels are just as valuable as those in the big leagues.

Finally, let me encourage each of you to do the best job you can, day in and day out. All of us have friends and coworkers who are seeing their fields being converted to artificial turf. In my area, it hurt to see the University of Missouri put in FieldTurf for the 2003 season. Each of us—sod growers, architects, agronomists, contractors and, especially, groundskeepers—must do a better job, and then some. In the last 50 years, and I have been a groundskeeper for 61 years, I have been trying very hard to improve the image of groundskeepers from "just a grass cutter" to a professional. Until the rake is plied from my cold dead fingers, I will always try to help dedicated groundskeepers, from preschool to the professional ranks, do the job, attain respect on all levels, and then some, which distinguishes the great from the mediocre.

Please, let's forget what happened in 2002 and move forward together, for our own sakes and for the sake of our profession. And may your good fortune be as numerous as the blades of grass.

Sincerely,

George P. Toma
July 2003